MW00344140

Mark

GlossaHouse Illustrated Greek-English New Testament

Mark

GlossaHouse Illustrated Greek-English New Testament

T. Michael W. Halcomb
Fredrick J. Long

GlossaHouse
Wilmore, KY
GH
www.GlossaHouse.com

GlossaHouse, LLC
110 Callis Circle
Wilmore, KY 40390

Mark: GlossaHouse Illustrated Greek-English New Testament

p. cm. — AGROS Series
ISBN-13: 978-0692206003
ISBN-10: 0692206000

The English translation of Mark used here, the GlossaHouse English Version (GEV), is original and has been created by T. Michael W. Halcomb and Fredrick J. Long.

The fonts used to create this work are available from www.linguistsoftware.com/lgku.htm.

Cover Design by T. Michael W. Halcomb
Book Design by T. Michael W. Halcomb
Updated Layout by T. Michael W. Halcomb
Illustration Design by Keith McNeely

AGROS

Accessible Greek Resources and Online Studies

AGROS

The Greek word ἀγρός is a field where seeds are planted and growth occurs. It can also denote a small village or community that forms around such a field. The type of community envisioned here is one that attends to Holy Scripture, particularly one that encourages the use of biblical Greek. Accessible Greek Resources and Online Studies (AGROS) is a tiered curriculum suite featuring innovative readers, grammars, specialized studies, and other exegetical resources to encourage and foster the exegetical use of biblical Greek. The goal of AGROS is to facilitate the creation and publication of innovative and inexpensive print and digital resources for the exposition of Scripture within the context of the global church. The AGROS curriculum includes five tiers, and each tier is indicated on the book's cover: Tier 1 (Beginning I), Tier 2 (Beginning II), Tier 3 (Intermediate I), Tier 4 (Intermediate II), and Tier 5 (Advanced). There are also two resource tracks: Conversational and Translational. Both involve intensive study of morphology, grammar, syntax, and discourse features. The conversational track specifically values the spoken word, and the enhanced learning associated with speaking a language in actual conversation. The translational track values the written word, and encourages analytical study to aide in understanding and translating biblical Greek and other Greek literature. The two resource tracks complement one another and can be pursued independently or together.

Table of Contents

Introduction

At the bottom of each page is the GlossaHouse English Version (GEV). This translation is fresh and fairly literal; we have attempted to preserve word order significance and accurately represent important features of the Greek text that are more emphasized and, therefore, more prominent. All of this was intended for the beginning student in mind, who may need help with Greek word meanings and understanding the significance of special constructions, like purpose, conditionals, and participles. In this translation work, we have applied current research on linguistics and Greek grammar, emphasis constructions, orality, performance, and social-cultural backgrounds. We have sought to strike a balance between trying to translate the import (as far as we can gather) of every sentence element but yet not "over" translating and moving into commentary. Understand that every translation always entails interpretation. We checked each other on a number of decisions, sometimes convincing the other of our particular views, sometimes not, on how best to translate some word, phrase or construction. In the end, we are quite confident in the results, knowing that there will be things that have been missed and points for improvement and enhancement. Let us comment on various features and aspects of this translation.

Greek Word Order is preserved as long as this still makes "good" English sense, especially when some sort of prominence attended the fronted word order. For example, preserving the preverbal placement of adverbial modifiers often retains their prominence in Greek. Additionally, because of this, the beginning and intermediate student will often be able to readily recognize where the English glosses are for words and phrases. For example, consider the preposed Οὕτως *thus* in Mark 4:26 (not translated in the NASB95, NLT, and ESV; but "This" in the NIV):

4:26 Καὶ ἔλεγεν· Οὕτως ἐστὶν ἡ βασιλεία τοῦ θεοῦ ὡς ἄνθρωπος βάλῃ τὸν σπόρον ἐπὶ τῆς γῆς
4:26 And he was saying, "Thus the kingdom of God is like a man who throws the seed on the ground…

However, this was not always possible, as in 10:23.

10:23 Καὶ περιβλεψάμενος ὁ Ἰησοῦς λέγει τοῖς μαθηταῖς αὐτοῦ· Πῶς δυσκόλως οἱ τὰ χρήματα ἔχοντες εἰς τὴν βασιλείαν τοῦ θεοῦ εἰσελεύσονται.
10:23 And, after looking around, Jesus says to his disciples, "How the ones having possessions will enter into the Kingdom of God with difficulty!"

The final position of "with difficulty" gives it due weight.

Implied words, most often objects of verbs and verbs, such as *it*, *him*, *them*, *is*, are often included in italics to help convey good English sense. The addition of such words was kept at a minimum; to place them in italics may reveals to readers where the Greek text may co-relate verbs by sharing the same objects, which may contribute to understanding the tone or atmosphere of the event or its description.

Gender Inclusiveness is preserved as much as possible. In his book, Art of the Start, revered businessman and author Guy Kawasaki once said of gender-inclusive language, "If only defeating sexism were as simple as throwing in an occasional he/she, she, her, or hers."[11] While Kawasaki goes on to use the pronoun "he" as a literary "shortcut," again, here we have attempted to preserve inclusiveness as much as possible. To cite Kawasaki again, he says, "Don't look for sexism where none exists." Thus, the Greek word ἄνθρωπος is most essentially a *human being* (BDAG 81.1), although often glossed and translated as "a man." Typically, ἄνθρωπος is translated as "a person" or in the plural "people."

Punctuation decisions are difficult. For imperatives and statements involving feeling, exclamation marks were used to help capture that tone and feeling. Also, we felt compelled at times to show different punctuation than found in SBL GNT; such decisions are interpretive. Students need to understand this. Here are a few examples to illustrate where and why we made these decisions.

1:27 καὶ ἐθαμβήθησαν ἅπαντες, ὥστε συζητεῖν πρὸς ἑαυτοὺς λέγοντας· Τί ἐστιν τοῦτο; διδαχὴ καινή·
κατ' ἐξουσίαν καὶ τοῖς πνεύμασι τοῖς ἀκαθάρτοις ἐπιτάσσει, καὶ ὑπακούουσιν αὐτῷ.
1:27 And all of them were amazed, so that they were discussing among themselves saying, "What is this? A
new teaching according to [God's] authority! Even to the unclean spirits he is giving orders, and they are
obeying him!"

The raised dot after διδαχὴ καινή· seems unwarranted, when the issue of "a new teaching" appears connected with "according to *God's* authority," presumably *God's* (hence, italics are used). This GEV punctuation is similar to the NIV and NLT, but not the NASB95 and ESV. What is accentuated by this punctuation is the next statement that begins with ascensive καί *even*. Here, too, exclamation marks are added to convey the tone of amazement and possibly surprise. Another very interpretive example is 2:27-28.

2:27 καὶ ἔλεγεν αὐτοῖς· Τὸ σάββατον διὰ τὸν ἄνθρωπον ἐγένετο καὶ οὐχ ὁ ἄνθρωπος διὰ τὸ σάββατον·
28 ὥστε κύριός ἐστιν ὁ υἱὸς τοῦ ἀνθρώπου καὶ τοῦ σαββάτου.
2:27 And he proceeded saying to them: "The Sabbath was made for humanity, and not humanity for the Sabbath." 28 As a result, then, the Son of Man is Lord even of the Sabbath.

The second verse is normally included within the quotation beginning in 2:27 as a statement of Jesus. However, as punctuated in the GEV, 2:28 is the narrator's interpretive voice, explaining the significance of Jesus's teaching on the Sabbath. Such a narrative voice occurs also in 7:19b about food laws in a parenthetical statement within a sentence: "(*He was* making all foods clean.)…." Another example occurs in 9:11.

9:11 καὶ ἐπηρώτων αὐτὸν λέγοντες· Ὅτι λέγουσιν οἱ γραμματεῖς ὅτι Ἠλίαν δεῖ ἐλθεῖν πρῶτον;
9:11 And they were questioning him saying this: "Are the scribes saying that Elijah must come first?"

In 9:11 the capitalized Ὅτι after a raised dot would indicate that the Ὅτι is included within the direct statement thus initiating a question, often translated "Why…?" (NIV, ESV, NLT; cf. NASB95). However, it seems better to understand here a recitative ὅτι after λέγοντες as occurs in 5:35, 8:28, 13:6, and 14:57-58. See further below on recitative ὅτι. Another example occurs in 12:16:

12:16 οἱ δὲ ἤνεγκαν. καὶ λέγει αὐτοῖς· <u>Τίνος ἡ εἰκὼν αὕτη</u> <u>καὶ ἡ ἐπιγραφή;</u> οἱ δὲ εἶπαν αὐτῷ· Καίσαρος.

12:16 So, they brought *it*. And he says to them, "<u>Whose *is* this image?</u> <u>And the inscription?</u>" So, they said to him, "Caesar's."

At issue is whether there are one or two questions. The αὕτη by proximity modifies ἡ εἰκὼν *image*, and oddly, isolates καὶ ἡ ἐπιγραφή suggesting that a second question occurs here with respect to the inscription with final emphasis. But why begin with the image, and then move to the inscription? In fact, the obverse image was of Tiberius Caesar (BMC 48; RIC 3), and around it was the inscription—the most relevant information (and most objectionable!) that identified its owner: *TI CAESAR DIVI AVG F AVGVSTVS*, which is translated: "Tiberius Caesar Augustus, Son of the divine/god Augustus." This later claim, that Augustus was "divine" or a "god," made the coin idolatrous for the Jews. It should be said that there was an image and inscription on the other side (reverse), but of a woman sitting (hard to identify) with the inscription *PONTIF MAXIM*, an abbreviation meaning "High Priest." So, two questions in Mark 12:16 seem likely: the first question identifies the observe side of the coin answering "Whose image is this?" (Tiberius Caesar's), and then the second question asks "Whose inscription?" on the obverse side of the coin, which specified in writing whose coin it was: Tiberius Caesar's.

Every Particle or **Conjunction** has been translated, including the very frequently occurring instances of καί and δέ. This has been a common fault of modern English Translations in general not to, sometimes with important interpretations at stake. Καί is marked +continuity but also +additive. When used adverbially as ascensive καί, this indicates additive emphasis and is often translated "also" or "even." Otherwise, καί is translated "and." The conjunction δέ is marked +new development, but can be used with contrasts (very context specific), but otherwise was translated so as to indicate movement in narrative. Thus, the following words have been used: *well*, *thus*, *moreover*, *additionally*, *but*, *so* (used in consequential narrative development is implied contextually), and occasionally *and*. In the case of μέν ... δέ, we avoided the common gloss *on the one hand... but on the other*, but we could not avoid it in Mark 16:19-20. The conjunction ἵνα, when indicating purpose, we have attempted to always render as *in order that*, which distinguishes it from result clauses (*so that*) or content clauses (*that*). However, there are instances where the sense of purpose, content, or result (much less common) were hard to distinguish (e.g., requests), so ἵνα may be translated simple as *that*. Finally, for purpose statements, since the notion of intention is pivotal, the English helping verb *would* is much preferable to *might* or *should*; this should be a corrective to learning that the subjunctive is a mood of possibility and can be translated with "might."

Second Person Subject Referents to Verbs are clearly indicated in especially two circumstances. First, when a singular subject governs the singular verb but then additional nominative subjects are indicated; in such a case, we might have expected a plural verb. Our strategy has been to translate the singular subject and verb first, and then place the additional nominative subjects in commas after the verb—this reflects the word order and the sense of priority on the singular subject. For example, consider 8:27a ἐξῆλθεν ὁ Ἰησοῦς καὶ οἱ μαθηταὶ αὐτοῦ εἰς τὰς κώμας Καισαρείας τῆς Φιλίππου· "Jesus went out, and his disciples, into the villages of Caesarea of Philip." Second, on occasions second person plural verbs are translated as "You *all*"—with the *all* in italics—in order to make it clear that a group is addressed and not one individual. This differs from when πάντες is present, which is translated "All of you" (with no italics). To mark the plural is sometimes very important, as in 14:37, for example, when somewhat surprisingly Jesus addresses Peter directly using the 2nd singular, but then in 14:38 switches to 2nd plural in the same speech act, which is otherwise unknown to English readers since it is indiscernible in major English translations (e.g., ESV, NASB95, NIV, NLT).

Verb Tenses in the Indicative Mood are translated somewhat consistently, with the most variation occurring with the Imperfect (see below). In light of the ongoing debate on the significance of the Greek verb and Verbal Aspect, we have taken a fairly conservative approach. We understand that imperfective verbal aspect (incomplete, in progress, internal) occurs in the Present and Imperfect Tenses, perfective aspect (complete or completed, external) in the Aorist Tense, stative/resultative aspect (complex action with effects) in the Perfect and Pluperfect Tenses, and future aspect (expectation) in the Future Tense. Our goal was to allow transparency in the translation; it is not that we think the translations are the best way to translate this or that verb in this or that context in every instance, but rather we wanted transparency in the English tense translation to the underlying Greek tenses, in order to facilitate observation, and further research and conversation. That being said, however, it is our current understanding that the augment in the Indicative moods marks past time, or possibly only remoteness; however, such remoteness would in narrative most often indicate past time.

<u>Present Tenses</u> are differentiated by the Historic Present (HP) in narrative description and by the Present Tense in direct or indirect conversation, because we wanted readers to see a simple present to demark the HP. If the Present Tense is used within direct discourse, then it is translated by the progressive English ("they are going"; "he is saying"). If the Present Tense occurs within indirect speech where typically Greek retains the original tense of the utterance—but this is not the English idiom—then the Present Tense is translated as if it were an Imperfect Tense, i.e. as progressive past tense ("He said that they were going…"). An interesting case occurs with 5:14b καὶ ἦλθον ἰδεῖν τί <u>ἐστιν</u> τὸ γεγονός. "And they came to see what it <u>was</u> that had happened." Here also the Perfect Tense substantive participle is translated as a pluperfect in English; but from the point of view of the utterance, the resultant effects were precisely the issue, τὸ γεγονός "what has happened." If used as a HP, then we retained the simple present tense ("they go"; "he says") in order to distinguish this from the Imperfect Tense, which is often translated as a progressive past ("they were going"; "he was saying").

<u>Imperfect Tense Verbs</u> are often translated as progressive past tense (they were going…). Mark uses several verbs to indicate amazement, which are not infrequently used in the Imperfect Tense. However, with verbs of emotional response, a past progressive translation was difficult to arrive at, since English verbs of emotional response or fear do not convey past progressive action. Consider the difference between "They were amazed-astonished" and "They were being amazed-astonished." One English verb that allowed past progressive sense was to marvel: "they were marveling…", which can also have an object. So, we used "was/were marveling" often (1:22; 2:12; 5:20; 6:2, etc.) or other strategies that would capture the incompleteness, as in 6:20 where the imperfect ἠπόρει is translated "he was remaining perplexed." With changes of setting, we have decided many times to translate such occurrences as inceptive (sometimes called ingressive): "began speaking." For example,

2:2 καὶ συνήχθησαν πολλοὶ ὥστε μηκέτι χωρεῖν μηδὲ τὰ πρὸς τὴν θύραν, καὶ <u>ἐλάλει</u> αὐτοῖς τὸν λόγον.

2:2 And many were gathered together, so that they could no longer make room, not even for those by the door, and he began speaking to them the word.

There were places where the Imperfect was translated "proceeded saying" when the imperfect is used within a conversational context or situation.

Future Tense Verbs are translated as simple futures ("they will go") unless otherwise needed, as, e.g. in an indirect question in 3:2: εἰ τοῖς σάββασιν θεραπεύσει αὐτόν "if on the Sabbath Days he would heal him." Here the original tense of the question is retained ("Will he heal him?") but this convention does not apply to English.

Aorist Tense Verbs are often translated as a simple past ("they went").

Perfect Tense Verbs are often translated as resultative ("they have gone").

Pluperfect Tense Verbs are translated as resultative in past time ("they had gone").

Non-Indicative Mood Verbs we have tried to render consistently, in order to, once again, promote observation and further research and conversation. For the Perfect Tense we attempted to convey a stative/resultative aspect (complex action with results); for the Present Tense, an imperfective aspect (in progress or incomplete); and for the Aorist Tense, a perfective aspect (complete or completed). These senses were sometimes quite difficult to convey and could easily encumber the translation.

Participles are complex to translate, since they occur in a variety of constructions. Moreover, participles are not inherently marked for any semantic relationship but the relationship must be discerned from broader context. Below are further discussions for translating participles, depending on their location and tense.

Pre-nuclear verb participles we translated as follows: when relative sequencing of events seemed the most basic relationship, then present tense participles are translated as contemporaneous ("while going along") and aorist tense participles as antecedent or time prior ("after going"). The same is generally true for Genitive Absolutes. If other such words were deemed necessary from contextual considerations to indicate special semantic relationship in English, these words (e.g., *thereby, by, although*) will be placed in italics to indicate their interpretive nature. A consistent exception is the aorist participle ἀποκριθεὶς, for which see further below.

Post-nuclear verb participles, since they tend to further describe the activity of the nuclear verb, were simply translated as participles ("seeing, walking"). Where the semantic relation from the semantics of the verb and context was so clear that the render it so generically strained English sense, then we supplied a conjunction in italics to indicate the semantic sense. For example, consider 15:30:

15:30 σῶσον σεαυτὸν καταβὰς ἀπὸ τοῦ σταυροῦ.

15:30 save yourself, *by* coming down from the cross!

Perfect tense participles represent special difficulty, but we have attempted to indicate resultant effects in other ways. For example, in 3:1 we see the Perfect Tense participle ἐξηραμμένην... τὴν χεῖρα "a completely withered up hand"; yet, in 3:3 the Aorist Tense participle is used of the same verb root uncompounded, which is simply τὴν χεῖρα ... ξηράν "the withered hand."

Imperatives and Infinitives were even more difficult to translate transparently showing verbal aspect. For example, translating the imperfective aspect as incomplete/progressive/internal for imperatives is often cumbersome. Mark 4:9 provides one poignant example of present infinitive and imperative:

4:9 Ὃς ἔχει ὦτα ἀκούειν ἀκουέτω. The one who has ears to be listening, be listening!

Various Types of Marked Constructions that convey some sort of emphasis were translated in such a way as to indicate their importance. Below is a brief accounting of these constructions, although this brief list does not nearly exhaust the different ways that Greek can indicate emphasis and give more prominence to sentences elements or discourse features; these latter, nevertheless, are hard to translate and often would have required extensive explanation.[2] More work is needed here; the following constructions were fairly clear to translate:

Fronted attributive demonstratives (i.e., placed in front of their head substantive) are foregrounded.[3] Consequently, we translated such instances using the adverb very. Consider 15:39b: Ἀληθῶς οὗτος ὁ ἄνθρωπος υἱὸς θεοῦ ἦν. "Truly this very person was the Son of God!"

Redundant nominative personal pronouns emphasize the subject, since the verbal endings are already mark subject person. Such redundancy is indicated by adding *–self* to the subject. So, in 3:11 one will find Σὺ εἶ ὁ υἱὸς τοῦ θεοῦ "You yourself are the Son of God!"

Emphatic negation with οὐ μή is often rendered *never ever* to capture the emphasis. Depending on the attending constructions, this is not always possible.

Rhetorical questions that indicate wither an expected affirmative or negative response are worded in such a way as to indicate as much, and then the response is placed within parentheses in italics with exclamation mark: (*No!*) or (*Surely, No!*) or (*Surely, yes!*). Remember the rule of MNOP: μή or μητί expects a negative answer (*Surely, No!*) and οὐ or οὐχί expects a positive answer (*Surely, yes!*). To see these rhetorical questions clearly in the English translation conveys the tone of disappointment, correction, surprise, or confrontation.

Recitative ὅτι is an optional phenomenon; direct speech may or may not be introduced by ὅτι. When ὅτι does occur, it likely sets off the statement for some discursive, pragmatic reason. Stephen H. Levinsohn proposes that it may help signal the culmination of an argument or, in John's Gospel, the explanation of previous teaching.[4] Most essentially, it would seem that recitative ὅτι is marked + prominence for introducing important direct speech, which may happen (often) to culminate a unit or explicate teaching. We have chosen to indicate the presence of recitative ὅτι by translating it with a near demonstrative pronoun "this: ...", because "this: ..." sets off and anticipates what follows formally in English. For example, consider 3:11-12 occurs near the end of a unit (which ends formally in 3:12; NASB95; ESV, NIV, etc.) in a generalizing statement.

3:11 καὶ τὰ πνεύματα τὰ ἀκάθαρτα, ὅταν αὐτὸν ἐθεώρουν, προσέπιπτον αὐτῷ καὶ ἔκραζον
λέγοντα ὅτι Σὺ εἶ ὁ υἱὸς τοῦ θεοῦ. 12 καὶ πολλὰ ἐπετίμα αὐτοῖς ἵνα μὴ αὐτὸν φανερὸν
ποιήσωσιν.

3:11 And the unclean spirits, whenever they were seeing him, were falling down before him and
were crying out saying this: "You yourself are the Son of God!" 12 And many times he was
rebuking them, in order that they would not make him known.

The Verb ἀποκρίνομαι, typically glossed as *I answer*, is used to mark participants taking back control or controlling the conversation. Levinsohn suggests that the use of the verb marks an attempt to control or take over the conversation. Therefore, we have chosen the gloss, *I answer back*, as is reflected in the translation. Such a decision augments one's understanding of the agonistic environment of challenge-riposte, and statement and response back, that this verb illustrates so well. Consider 3:32-33:

3:32 καὶ ἐκάθητο περὶ αὐτὸν ὄχλος, καὶ λέγουσιν αὐτῷ· Ἰδοὺ ἡ μήτηρ σου καὶ οἱ ἀδελφοί
σου ἔξω ζητοῦσίν σε. 33 καὶ ἀποκριθεὶς αὐτοῖς λέγει· Τίς ἐστιν ἡ μήτηρ μου ἢ οἱ
ἀδελφοί μου;

3:32 And a crowd was sitting around him and they say to him, "Behold, your mother and your
brothers are outside seeking you." 33 And answering back to them, he says, "Who is my mother
or my brothers?"

The Affirmative ἀμήν *amen* we have understood as backward referencing to the previous speech or actions. Such an understanding comports with its liturgical backward referencing in Hebrew Scripture, to affirm what has been said (BDAG 53.1a). This is quite a different way of understanding ἀμήν in Jesus's usage with verbs of sayings, which is typically translated "Truly I say to you…" and pointing forward "beginning a solemn declaration but used only by Jesus" (BDAG 53.1b.). But since the adverb ἀληθῶς is also glossed and translated as "truly" (see Mark 15:39b above), we decided to translate ἀμήν "Amen!" It is worth considering how the ἀμήν affirms what has been said or has happened and then is conjoined with forward pointing statements of "saying."

Pronunciation might seem like somewhat of an odd feature to include here but it is worthy of mention because it comes to bear on transliteration. Here is an example of how the Aramaic of Mk 15:34 has been transliterated in the GEV:

15:34 καὶ τῇ ἐνάτῃ ὥρᾳ ἐβόησεν ὁ Ἰησοῦς φωνῇ μεγάλῃ· Ἐλωῒ ἐλωῒ λεμὰ σαβαχθάνι; ὅ ἐστιν
μεθερμηνευόμενον Ὁ θεός μου ὁ θεός μου, εἰς τί ἐγκατέλιπές με;

15:34 And at the ninth hour Jesus cried with a loud voice, "Eloi, Eloi, lema savakhthani," which is
translated: 'My God, my God, why did you abandon me?'"

The traditional transliteration of the term σαβαχθάνι is *sabachthani*. Two points of difference arise here with the GEV: The Greek letter β is rendered with an English "v" instead of "b" and the Greek letter χ is rendered with "kh" instead of "ch". This transliteration is based on the so-called Erasmian pronunciation, which is popular in the Western academic world, but is ultimately anachronistic and flawed. Thus, in spite of the myth that the pronunciation of Koine Greek cannot be recovered, we believe it can. Ultimately, this has bearing on how we go about the task of transliteration. It is our view that it is much more helpful if students, especially beginning students, are able to include correct historical approximations of sound in a letter-for-letter format when transliterating. Much more could be said about this matter but such is beyond the scope of this work.[5] We have, however, included a table on the following page to assist with matters of pronunciation and transliteration.[6]

---

1. Guy Kawasaki, *The Art of the Start: The Time-Tested, Battle-Hardened Guide for Anyone Starting Anything* (Penguin: New York, 2004), 5 fn1.

2. See the following two forthcoming works by Fredrick J. Long: *A Beginning Exegetical and Discourse Grammar* (Wilmore, Ky.: GlossaHouse, 2014) *forthcoming* and *2 Corinthians: A Handbook on the Greek Text* (Baylor Handbook on the Greek New Testament; Waco, Tex.: Baylor University Press, 2014).

3. Stanley E. Porter, "Prominence: An Overview," in *The Linguist as Pedagogue: Trends in the Teaching and Linguistic Analysis of the Greek New Testament* (ed. Stanley E. Porter and Matthew Brook O'Donnell; New Testament Monographs 11; Sheffield: Sheffield Phoenix, 2009), 45–74 at 68.

4. Stephen H. Levinsohn has been interested in describing the discourse pragmatic function of ὅτι in narrative with verbs of saying (*Discourse Features of New Testament Greek: A Coursebook on the Information Structure of New Testament Greek* [2nd ed.; Dallas: Summer Institute of Linguistics, 2000] ch.16). His conclusions are that in John and Luke-Acts such explicit use of ὅτι occurs at the culmination of a unit or sub-unit, i.e., the ὅτι will "signal that the quotation it introduces culminates an argument" (269). He also notes that in Luke's and John's Gospel the statement Ἀμὴν ἀμὴν λέγω ὑμῖν/σοι "Truly, truly I say to you," when followed by ὅτι, is used to explicate previous teaching. See also Levinsohn, "Ὅτι Recitativum in John's Gospel: A Stylistic or a Pragmatic Device?," *Working Papers of the Summer Institute of Linguistics, University of North Dakota Session 43* (1999): 1-14. Online: http://www.und.edu/dept/linguistics/wp/1999Levinsohn.PDF.

5. See T. Michael W. Halcomb, "Never Trust a Greek…Professor: Revisiting the Question of How Koine Was Pronounced" (paper presented at the annual Stone-Campbell Journal Conference, Johnson City, Tn., 14 March 2014) and "Pronouncing Koine Greek(,) A Dead Language: Issues Concerning Orality, Morality, and the Pronunciation of Koine Greek" (paper presented at the annual Theological Educators Forum on Orality, Wilmore, Ky., 14 April 2014).

6. Taken from Halcomb, "Never Trust" (13).

Koine Era Pronunciation (KEP)

Alphabet

Letters	*Transliteration Value*	*Pronunciation (Approx. English Value/Sound)*	*Examples of Greek Words Transliterated*
Α, α	A, a	ah – torah	λαμβάνω lamvanō
Β, β	V, v	v – yet	λαμβάνω lamvanō
Γ, γ	Y, y – before ε, ι, and ει Gh, gh – before other vowels	y – yet gh – ghost (but a bit softer)	ἅγιος ayiōs ἀγαθός aghathōs
Δ, δ	Dh, dh or Th, th	dh – the (no Eng. equiv.) th - the	διά dhia thia
Ε, ε	E, e	eh – mikveh	σέ, se
Ζ, ζ	Z, z	z – zoo	ζῷον, zōōn
Η, η	Ā, ā	āy – pay	μή, mā
Θ, θ	Th, th	th – think	θεός, theōs
Ι, ι	I, i Y, y	ee – beet y – yes (often will begin words)	Ἰησοῦς Yāysous
Κ, κ	K, k	k – key	καί, kai
Λ, λ	L, l	l – leg	λέγω, legō
Μ, μ	M, m	m – mad	μέν, men
Ν, ν	N, n	n – no	νῦν, nyn
Ξ, ξ	Ks, ks	ks – books	ξένος, ksenōs
Ο, ο	Ō, ō	ō – go	πρός, prōs
Π, π	P, p	p – peek	παῖς, pais
Ρ, ρ	R, r	r – rim (trill/roll)	ῥίζα, riza
Σ, σ, ς	S, s	s – sit	σοῦ, sou
Τ, τ	T, t	t – tip	τίς, tis
Υ, υ	Y, y V, v – in diphthongs following α, ε, η (i.e. αυ, ευ, ηυ)	eew – au jus (cf. οι) av – avocado (αυ) ev – every (ευ) āv – āvery (ηυ)	κύριος kyriōs (see diphthongs for examples of these)
Φ, φ	F, f (or Ph, ph)	f – fit	φάγε, fage
Χ, χ	Kh, kh (or X, x)	kh – backhoe (slight guttural)	χάρις kharis
Ψ, ψ	Ps, ps	ps – psalm	ψώρα, psōra
Ω, ω	Ō, ō	ō – go	ᾠόν, ōōn

Diphthongs

Letters	*Transliteration Value*	*Pronunciation (Approx. English Value/Sound)*
αι	ai	ai (= eh) – said
αυ	av, af (before β, δ, γ, λ, μ, ν, ρ, ζ)	av – avocado af - waft
ει	ei	ee – beet
ευ	ev, ef (before β, δ, γ, λ, μ, ν, ρ, ζ)	ev – every ef - left
ηυ	āv, āf (before β, δ, γ, λ, μ, ν, ρ, ζ)	āv – āvery āf – sāfe
οι	oi	like "eew" in "jus" of French "au jus"
ου	ou	ou – coup
υι	ui	iy – teriyaki

Consonant Clusters

γγ	ng	ng - hang
γκ	nk	nk - dunk
γχ	nkh	nkh - ankh
γξ	nks	nks - thanks
μβ	mv	mv - humvee
ντ	nt	nt - ant or: nd - and

Note: While the rough breathing mark is denoted in writing (e.g. `H, h`.), there is no "rough breathing" sound (e.g. the voiced "h" in "ha" or "help") articulated in the Koine Era Pronunciation. This is because aspiration (i.e. the so-called rough breathing) had fallen out of use hundreds of years prior to the Koine/Hellenistic era. In spite of this fact, Erasmian continues to use it.

Κεφ. Α´
1 Ἀρχὴ τοῦ εὐαγγελίου Ἰησοῦ χριστοῦ [υἱοῦ τοῦ θεοῦ]
2 Καθὼς γέγραπται ἐν τῷ Ἠσαΐᾳ τῷ προφήτῃ·
Ἰδοὺ ἀποστέλλω τὸν ἄγγελόν μου πρὸ προσώπου σου, ὃς κατασκευάσει τὴν ὁδόν σου·
3 φωνὴ βοῶντος ἐν τῇ ἐρήμῳ· Ἑτοιμάσατε τὴν ὁδὸν κυρίου, εὐθείας ποιεῖτε τὰς τρίβους αὐτοῦ,
4 ἐγένετο Ἰωάννης ὁ βαπτίζων ἐν τῇ ἐρήμῳ κηρύσσων βάπτισμα μετανοίας εἰς ἄφεσιν ἁμαρτιῶν.
5 καὶ ἐξεπορεύετο πρὸς αὐτὸν πᾶσα ἡ Ἰουδαία χώρα καὶ οἱ Ἱεροσολυμῖται πάντες, καὶ ἐβαπτίζοντο ὑπ᾽ αὐτοῦ ἐν τῷ Ἰορδάνῃ ποταμῷ ἐξομολογούμενοι τὰς ἁμαρτίας αὐτῶν.
6 καὶ ἦν ὁ Ἰωάννης ἐνδεδυμένος τρίχας καμήλου καὶ ζώνην δερματίνην περὶ τὴν ὀσφὺν αὐτοῦ, καὶ ἔσθων ἀκρίδας καὶ μέλι ἄγριον.
7 καὶ ἐκήρυσσεν λέγων·
Ἔρχεται ὁ ἰσχυρότερός μου ὀπίσω μου, οὗ οὐκ εἰμὶ ἱκανὸς κύψας λῦσαι τὸν ἱμάντα τῶν ὑποδημάτων αὐτοῦ· 8 ἐγὼ ἐβάπτισα ὑμᾶς ὕδατι, αὐτὸς δὲ βαπτίσει ὑμᾶς ἐν πνεύματι ἁγίῳ.

1:1 The beginning of the gospel of Jesus Christ, the Son of God. 2 Just as it has been written in Isaiah the prophet, "Behold, I am sending my messenger before your face,
who will prepare your way, 3 a voice of one crying in the wilderness, 'Prepare the way of the Lord, make his paths straight.'" 4 John came, the one baptizing in the
wilderness, preaching a baptism of repentance for the forgiveness of sins. 5 And going out to him was all the Judean countryside and all the Jerusalemites, and they were
being baptized by him in the Jordan River confessing their sins. 6 And John was wearing camel's hair and a leather belt around his waist, and eating locusts and wild
honey. 7 And he kept preaching saying, "The One mightier than me is coming after me, whose strap of his sandals I am not worthy to stoop down to untie. 8 I myself
baptized you with water, but he himself will baptize you in the Holy Spirit."

9 Καὶ ἐγένετο ἐν ἐκείναις ταῖς ἡμέραις ἦλθεν Ἰησοῦς ἀπὸ Ναζαρὲτ τῆς Γαλιλαίας καὶ ἐβαπτίσθη εἰς τὸν Ἰορδάνην ὑπὸ Ἰωάννου. 10 καὶ εὐθὺς ἀναβαίνων ἐκ τοῦ ὕδατος εἶδεν σχιζομένους τοὺς οὐρανοὺς καὶ τὸ πνεῦμα ὡς περιστερὰν καταβαῖνον εἰς αὐτόν·

11 καὶ φωνὴ ἐγένετο ἐκ τῶν οὐρανῶν·
Σὺ εἶ ὁ υἱός μου ὁ ἀγαπητός, ἐν σοὶ εὐδόκησα.

12 Καὶ εὐθὺς τὸ πνεῦμα αὐτὸν ἐκβάλλει εἰς τὴν ἔρημον.

13 καὶ ἦν ἐν τῇ ἐρήμῳ τεσσεράκοντα ἡμέρας πειραζόμενος ὑπὸ τοῦ Σατανᾶ, καὶ ἦν μετὰ τῶν θηρίων, καὶ οἱ ἄγγελοι διηκόνουν αὐτῷ.

14 Καὶ μετὰ τὸ παραδοθῆναι τὸν Ἰωάννην ἦλθεν ὁ Ἰησοῦς εἰς τὴν Γαλιλαίαν κηρύσσων τὸ εὐαγγέλιον τοῦ θεοῦ 15 καὶ λεγων ὅτι

Πεπλήρωται ὁ καιρὸς καὶ ἤγγικεν ἡ βασιλεία τοῦ θεοῦ· μετανοεῖτε καὶ πιστεύετε ἐν τῷ εὐαγγελίῳ.

16 Καὶ παράγων παρὰ τὴν θάλασσαν τῆς Γαλιλαίας εἶδεν Σίμωνα καὶ Ἀνδρέαν τὸν ἀδελφὸν Σίμωνος ἀμφιβάλλοντας ἐν τῇ θαλάσσῃ, ἦσαν γὰρ ἁλιεῖς·
17 καὶ εἶπεν αὐτοῖς ὁ Ἰησοῦς·

Δεῦτε ὀπίσω μου, καὶ ποιήσω ὑμᾶς γενέσθαι ἁλιεῖς ἀνθρώπων.

18 καὶ εὐθὺς ἀφέντες τὰ δίκτυα ἠκολούθησαν αὐτῷ.
19 καὶ προβὰς ὀλίγον εἶδεν Ἰάκωβον τὸν τοῦ Ζεβεδαίου καὶ Ἰωάννην τὸν ἀδελφὸν αὐτοῦ, καὶ αὐτοὺς ἐν τῷ πλοίῳ καταρτίζοντας τὰ δίκτυα,
20 καὶ εὐθὺς ἐκάλεσεν αὐτούς. καὶ ἀφέντες τὸν πατέρα αὐτῶν Ζεβεδαῖον ἐν τῷ πλοίῳ μετὰ τῶν μισθωτῶν ἀπῆλθον ὀπίσω αὐτοῦ.

9 And it happened in those days, Jesus came from Nazareth of Galilee and was baptized in the Jordan by John. 10 And straightaway while coming up out of the water, he
saw the heavens being ripped open and the Spirit like a dove descending on him. 11 And a voice came out of the heavens, "You yourself are my beloved Son; with you I
am pleased." 12 And immediately the Spirit casts him out into the wilderness. 13 And he was in the wilderness forty days being tempted by Satan, and he was with the wild
beasts, and the angels were ministering to him. 14 And after John was delivered up, Jesus came into Galilee preaching the gospel of God, 15 and saying this: "The time has
been fulfilled and the kingdom of God has come near; repent and believe in the gospel." 16 And while passing along besides the Sea of Galilee, he saw Simon and Andrew,
the brother of Simon, casting *a net* in the sea, for they were fishermen. 17 And Jesus said to them, "Come behind me, and I will make you become fishers of people."
18 And immediately after leaving the nets, they followed him. 19 And after going on a little farther, he saw Jacob the *son* of Zebedee and John his brother, and them in the
boat readying the nets. 20 And straightaway he called them. And after leaving their father Zebedee in the boat with the hired workers, they departed behind him.

21 Καὶ εἰσπορεύονται εἰς Καφαρναούμ. καὶ εὐθὺς τοῖς σάββασιν ἐδίδασκεν εἰς τὴν συναγωγήν.
22 καὶ ἐξεπλήσσοντο ἐπὶ τῇ διδαχῇ αὐτοῦ, ἦν γὰρ διδάσκων αὐτοὺς ὡς ἐξουσίαν ἔχων καὶ οὐχ ὡς οἱ γραμματεῖς.
23 καὶ εὐθὺς ἦν ἐν τῇ συναγωγῇ αὐτῶν ἄνθρωπος ἐν πνεύματι ἀκαθάρτῳ καὶ ἀνέκραξεν 24 λέγων·

Τί ἡμῖν καὶ σοί, Ἰησοῦ Ναζαρηνέ; ἦλθες ἀπολέσαι ἡμᾶς; οἶδά σε τίς εἶ, ὁ ἅγιος τοῦ θεοῦ.

25 καὶ ἐπετίμησεν αὐτῷ ὁ Ἰησοῦς λέγων·
Φιμώθητι καὶ ἔξελθε ἐξ αὐτοῦ.
26 καὶ σπαράξαν αὐτὸν τὸ πνεῦμα τὸ ἀκάθαρτον καὶ φωνῆσαν φωνῇ μεγάλη ἐξῆλθεν ἐξ αὐτοῦ.

27 καὶ ἐθαμβήθησαν ἅπαντες, ὥστε συζητεῖν πρὸς ἑαυτοὺς λέγοντας·
Τί ἐστιν τοῦτο; διδαχὴ καινή· κατ’ ἐξουσίαν καὶ τοῖς πνεύμασι τοῖς ἀκαθάρτοις ἐπιτάσσει, καὶ ὑπακούουσιν αὐτῷ.
28 καὶ ἐξῆλθεν ἡ ἀκοὴ αὐτοῦ εὐθὺς πανταχοῦ εἰς ὅλην τὴν περίχωρον τῆς Γαλιλαίας.

[21] And they enter into Capernaum. And straightaway on the Sabbath Days he was teaching in the synagogue. [22] And they were marveling at his teaching, for he was
teaching them like one having authority and not like the scribes. [23] And suddenly there was in their synagogue a person with an unclean spirit and he cried out [24] saying,
"What do our affairs *have to do* with yours, Jesus, Nazarene? Have you come to destroy us? I know you, who you are, the Holy One of God." [25] And Jesus rebuked him
saying, "Be quiet and come out of him!" [26] And the unclean spirit, after shaking him and crying out with a loud sound, came out from him. [27] And all of them were amazed,
so that they were discussing among themselves saying, "What is this? A new teaching according to *God's* authority! Even to the unclean spirits he is giving orders, and
they are obeying him!" [28] And the news about him went out immediately everywhere into the whole region of Galilee.

29 Καὶ εὐθὺς ἐκ
τῆς συναγωγῆς
ἐξελθόντες ἦλ-
θον εἰς τὴν οἰ-
κίαν Σίμωνος
καὶ Ἀνδρέου με-
τὰ Ἰακώβου καὶ
Ἰωάννου.
30 ἡ δὲ πενθερὰ Σί-
μωνος κατέκειτο πυ-
ρέσσουσα, καὶ εὐθὺς
λέγουσιν αὐτῷ περὶ
αὐτῆς.
31 καὶ προσελθὼν ἤγ-
ειρεν αὐτὴν κρατήσας
τῆς χειρός· καὶ ἀφῆ-
κεν αὐτὴν ὁ πυρετός,
καὶ διηκόνει αὐτοῖς.

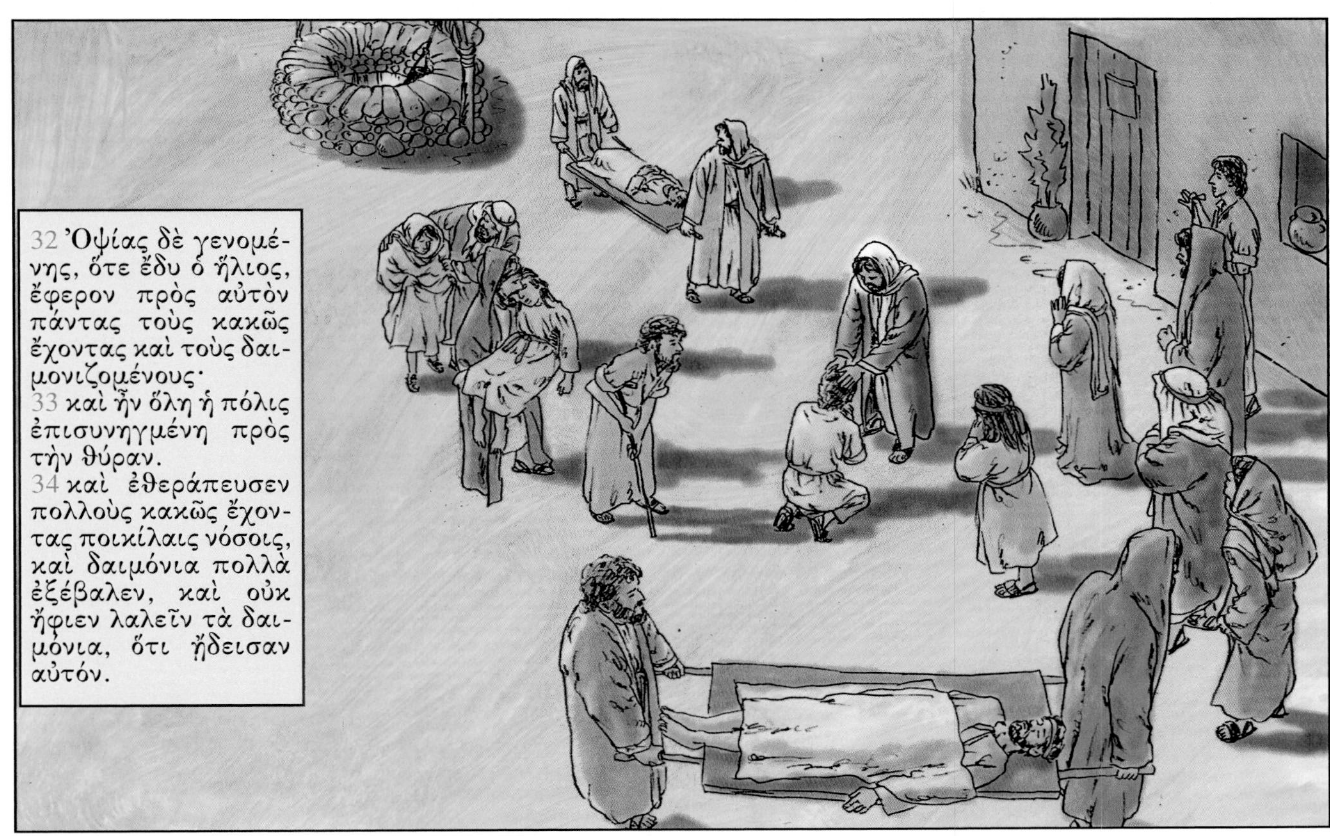

32 Ὀψίας δὲ γενομέ-
νης, ὅτε ἔδυ ὁ ἥλιος,
ἔφερον πρὸς αὐτὸν
πάντας τοὺς κακῶς
ἔχοντας καὶ τοὺς δαι-
μονιζομένους·
33 καὶ ἦν ὅλη ἡ πόλις
ἐπισυνηγμένη πρὸς
τὴν θύραν.
34 καὶ ἐθεράπευσεν
πολλοὺς κακῶς ἔχον-
τας ποικίλαις νόσοις,
καὶ δαιμόνια πολλὰ
ἐξέβαλεν, καὶ οὐκ
ἤφιεν λαλεῖν τὰ δαι-
μόνια, ὅτι ᾔδεισαν
αὐτόν.

35 Καὶ πρωῒ ἔννυχα
λίαν ἀναστὰς ἐξ-
ῆλθεν καὶ ἀπῆλθεν
εἰς ἔρημον τόπον
κἀκεῖ προσηύχετο.
36 καὶ κατεδίωξεν
αὐτὸν Σίμων καὶ οἱ
μετ' αὐτοῦ,
37 καὶ εὗρον αὐτὸν
καὶ λέγουσιν αὐτῷ
ὅτι
Πάντες ζητοῦσίν σε.

29 And immediately after exiting from the synagogue, they went into the house of Simon and Andrew with James and John. 30 Well, the mother-in-law of Simon was lying
down burning up *in a fever*, and straightaway they begin speaking to him about her. 31 And after approaching, he raised her up, having grasped the hand; and the fever left
her, and she was ministering to them. 32 Well, after it became late, when the sun went down, they kept carrying to him all the ones doing poorly and the ones being
possessed by demons. 33 And the whole city was gathering at the door. 34 And he healed many doing poorly with various diseases, and he cast out many demons and he
was not permitting the demons to speak, because they knew him. 35 And very early in the morning, after getting up, he went out and departed into a desolate place and
there he was praying. 36 And Simon searched for him, and those with him, 37 and they found him and they begin saying to him this: "They all are seeking you!"

Ἄγωμεν ἀλλαχοῦ εἰς τὰς ἐχομένας κωμοπόλεις, ἵνα καὶ ἐκεῖ κηρύξω, εἰς τοῦτο γὰρ ἐξῆλθον.

39 καὶ ἦλθεν κηρύσσων εἰς τὰς συναγωγὰς αὐτῶν εἰς ὅλην τὴν Γαλιλαίαν καὶ τὰ δαιμόνια ἐκβάλλων.

40 Καὶ ἔρχεται πρὸς αὐτὸν λεπρὸς παρακαλῶν αὐτὸν καὶ γονυπετῶν λέγων αὐτῷ ὅτι
Ἐὰν θέλῃς δύνασαί με καθαρίσαι.

41 καὶ ὀργισθεὶς ἐκτείνας τὴν χεῖρα αὐτοῦ ἥψατο καὶ λέγει αὐτῷ·

Θέλω, καθαρίσθητι·

42 καὶ εὐθὺς ἀπῆλθεν ἀπ᾽ αὐτοῦ ἡ λέπρα, καὶ ἐκαθαρίσθη.
43 καὶ ἐμβριμησάμενος αὐτῷ εὐθὺς ἐξέβαλεν αὐτόν,
44 καὶ λέγει αὐτῷ·
Ὅρα μηδενὶ μηδὲν εἴπῃς, ἀλλὰ ὕπαγε σεαυτὸν δεῖξον τῷ ἱερεῖ καὶ προσένεγκε περὶ τοῦ καθαρισμοῦ σου ἃ προσέταξεν Μωϋσῆς εἰς μαρτύριον αὐτοῖς.
45 ὁ δὲ ἐξελθὼν ἤρξατο κηρύσσειν πολλὰ καὶ διαφημίζειν τὸν λόγον, ὥστε μηκέτι αὐτὸν δύνασθαι φανερῶς εἰς πόλιν εἰσελθεῖν, ἀλλὰ ἔξω ἐπ᾽ ἐρήμοις τόποις ἦν· καὶ ἤρχοντο πρὸς αὐτὸν πάντοθεν.

Κεφ.
Β´

1 Καὶ εἰσελθὼν πάλιν εἰς Καφαρναοὺμ δι᾽ ἡμερῶν ἠκούσθη ὅτι ἐν οἴκῳ ἐστίν·
2 καὶ συνήχθησαν πολλοὶ ὥστε μηκέτι χωρεῖν μηδὲ τὰ πρὸς τὴν θύραν, καὶ ἐλάλει αὐτοῖς τὸν λόγον.

[38] And he says to them, “Let us go elsewhere into the nearby towns, in order that also there I would preach. For I came out *here* for this reason.” [39] And he went preaching
in their synagogues in the whole of Galilee and casting out demons. [40] And a leper comes to him, calling him and kneeling, saying to him this: “If you want, you are able
to cleanse me.” [41] And angered, stretching out the hand, he touched him and says to him, “I want, be cleansed!” [42] And immediately the leprosy departed from him, and
he was made clean. [43] And after sternly ordering him, immediately he cast him away, [44] and he says to him, “See no one! Say nothing! But go, show yourself to the priest
and offer concerning your cleansing that which Moses commanded for a testimony to them.” [45] Well, he, after going out, began to preach many things and to spread the
word, so that he was no longer able openly to enter into a city, but he was outside in the desolate places. And they were coming to him from everywhere. 2:1 And after
entering again into Capernaum after several days, it was heard that he was in a house. [2] And many were gathered together, so that they could no longer make room, not
even for those by the door, and he began speaking to them the word.

3 καὶ ἔρχονται φέροντες πρὸς αὐτὸν παραλυτικὸν αἰρόμενον ὑπὸ τεσσάρων.
4 καὶ μὴ δυνάμενοι προσενέγκαι αὐτῷ διὰ τὸν ὄχλον ἀπεστέγασαν τὴν στέγην ὅπου ἦν,

καὶ ἐξορύξαντες χαλῶσι τὸν κράβαττον ὅπου ὁ παραλυτικὸς κατέκειτο.
5 καὶ ἰδὼν ὁ Ἰησοῦς τὴν πίστιν αὐτῶν λέγει τῷ παραλυτικῷ·
Τέκνον, ἀφίενταί σου αἱ ἁμαρτίαι.
6 ἦσαν δέ τινες τῶν γραμματέων ἐκεῖ καθήμενοι καὶ διαλογιζόμενοι ἐν ταῖς καρδίαις αὐτῶν·
7 Τί οὗτος οὕτως λαλεῖ; βλασφημεῖ· τίς δύναται ἀφιέναι ἁμαρτίας εἰ μὴ εἷς ὁ θεός;

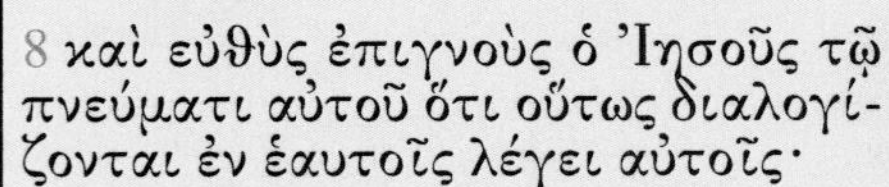
8 καὶ εὐθὺς ἐπιγνοὺς ὁ Ἰησοῦς τῷ πνεύματι αὐτοῦ ὅτι οὕτως διαλογίζονται ἐν ἑαυτοῖς λέγει αὐτοῖς·

Τί ταῦτα διαλογίζεσθε ἐν ταῖς καρδίαις ὑμῶν;
9 τί ἐστιν εὐκοπώ-τερον, εἰπεῖν τῷ παραλυτικῷ· Ἀφίεν-ταί σου αἱ ἁμαρτίαι, ἢ εἰπεῖν· Ἔγειρε καὶ ἆρον τὸν κράβαττόν σου καὶ περιπάτει;
10 ἵνα δὲ εἰδῆτε ὅτι ἐξουσίαν ἔχει ὁ υἱὸς τοῦ ἀνθρώπου ἐπὶ τῆς γῆς ἀφιέναι ἁμαρτίας—

λέγει τῷ παραλυτικῷ·
11 Σοὶ λέγω, ἔγειρε ἆρον τὸν κράβαττόν σου καὶ ὕπαγε εἰς τὸν οἶκόν σου.

3 And they come carrying to him a paralytic being lifted by four people. 4 And not being able to bring *him* to him because of the crowd, they unroofed the roof where he
was, and, after digging through, they lower the bed where the paralytic was lying. 5 And Jesus, after seeing their faith, says to the paralytic, “Child, your sins are forgiven.”
6 But there were some scribes there sitting and reasoning in their hearts, 7 “Why is this man speaking this way? He is blaspheming! Who is able to forgive sins except one,
namely, God?” 8 And straightaway, Jesus, after perceiving in his spirit that they were debating within themselves, says to them, “Why are you debating these things in
your hearts? 9 What is easier, to say to the paralytic, ‘Your sins are forgiven,’ or to say, ‘Start getting up and take up your bed and keep walking!’? 10 But in order that you
would know that the Son of Man has authority upon the earth to forgive sins” - he says to the paralytic: 11 “I say to you, ‘Start getting up, take up your bed, and get going
to your house.’”

καὶ ἠγέρθη καὶ εὐθὺς ἄρας τὸν κράβαττον ἐξῆλθεν ἔμπροσθεν πάντων, ὥστε ἐξίστασθαι πάντας καὶ δοξάζειν τὸν θεὸν λέγοντας ὅτι

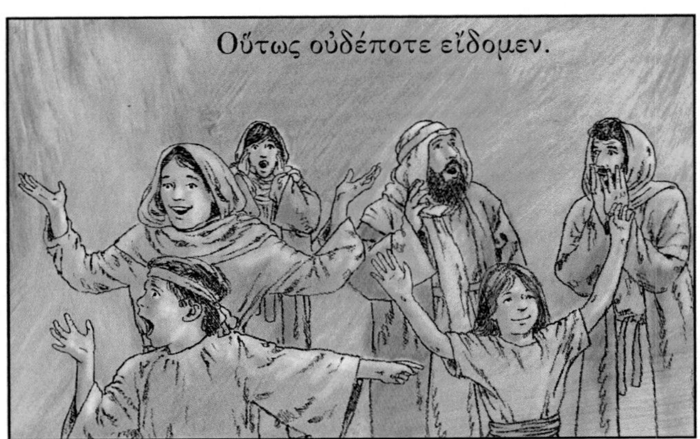
Οὕτως οὐδέποτε εἴδομεν.

13 Καὶ ἐξῆλθεν πάλιν παρὰ τὴν θάλασσαν· καὶ πᾶς ὁ ὄχλος ἤρχετο πρὸς αὐτόν, καὶ ἐδίδασκεν αὐτούς.

14 καὶ παράγων εἶδεν Λευὶν τὸν τοῦ Ἁλφαίου καθήμενον ἐπὶ τὸ τελώνιον, καὶ λέγει αὐτῷ·
Ἀκολούθει μοι.
καὶ ἀναστὰς ἠκολούθησεν αὐτῷ.
15 Καὶ γίνεται κατακεῖσθαι αὐτὸν ἐν τῇ οἰκίᾳ αὐτοῦ, καὶ πολλοὶ τελῶναι καὶ ἁμαρτωλοὶ συνανέκειντο τῷ Ἰησοῦ καὶ τοῖς μαθηταῖς αὐτοῦ, ἦσαν γὰρ πολλοὶ καὶ ἠκολούθουν αὐτῷ.

16 καὶ οἱ γραμματεῖς τῶν Φαρισαίων ἰδόντες ὅτι ἐσθίει μετὰ τῶν ἁμαρτωλῶν καὶ τελωνῶν ἔλεγον τοῖς μαθηταῖς αὐτοῦ·
Ὅτι μετὰ τῶν τελωνῶν καὶ ἁμαρτωλῶν ἐσθίει;

[12] And he arose, and straightaway, after taking up the bed, he went out before them all, so that all were marveling and were glorifying God saying this: "We have never seen *anything* such as this!" [13] And he went out again along the sea; and all the crowd began coming to him, and he was teaching them. [14] And while going along, he saw Levi the *son* of Alphaeus sitting at the toll booth, and he says to him, "Follow me." And after arising, he followed him. [15] And it happens that he sits with him in his house, and many tax collectors and sinners were sitting with Jesus and his disciples, for there were many, and they began following him. [16] And the scribes of the Pharisees, after seeing that he was eating with the sinners and tax collectors, began saying to his disciples, "Why, with the tax collectors and sinners, is he eating?"

17 καὶ ἀκούσας ὁ Ἰησοῦς λέγει αὐ-τοῖς ὅτι
Οὐ χρείαν ἔχουσιν οἱ ἰσχύοντες ἰατροῦ ἀλλ' οἱ κακῶς ἔχοντες· οὐκ ἦλθον καλέσαι δικαίους ἀλλὰ ἁμαρτωλούς.
18 Καὶ ἦσαν οἱ μαθηταὶ Ἰωάννου καὶ οἱ Φαρι-σαῖοι νηστεύοντες. καὶ ἔρχονται καὶ λέγουσιν αὐτῷ·
Διὰ τί οἱ μαθηταὶ Ἰωάννου καὶ οἱ μαθηταὶ τῶν Φαρισαίων νηστεύουσιν, οἱ δὲ σοὶ μαθηταὶ οὐ νηστεύουσιν;

19 καὶ εἶπεν αὐτοῖς ὁ Ἰησοῦς·
Μὴ δύνανται οἱ υἱοὶ τοῦ νυμφῶνος ἐν ᾧ ὁ νυμφίος μετ' αὐτῶν ἐστιν νηστεύειν; ὅσον χρό-νον ἔχουσιν τὸν νυμφίον μετ' αὐτῶν οὐ δύνανται νηστεύειν·
20 ἐλεύσονται δὲ ἡμέραι ὅταν ἀπαρθῇ ἀπ' αὐτῶν ὁ νυμφίος, καὶ τότε νηστεύσουσιν ἐν ἐκείνῃ τῇ ἡμέρᾳ.

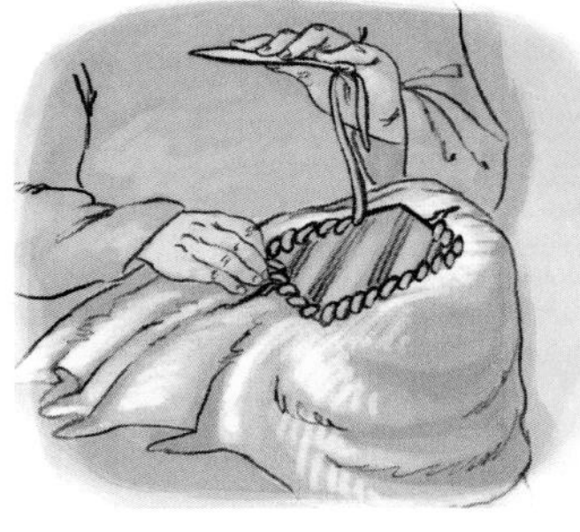
21 Οὐδεὶς ἐπίβλημα ῥάκους ἀγνάφου ἐπιράπτει εἰ δὲ μή,

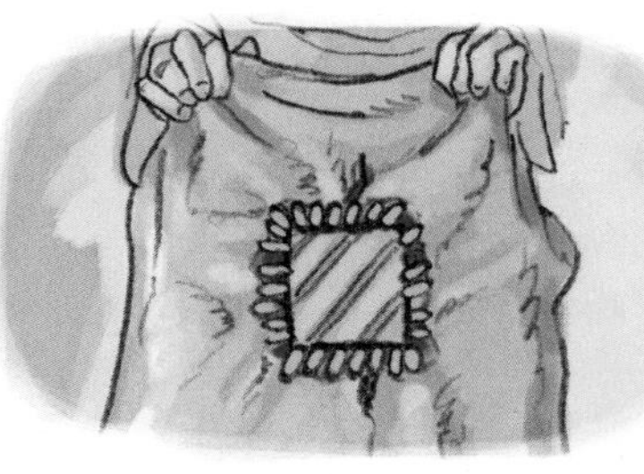
αἴρει τὸ πλήρωμα ἀπ' αὐτοῦ τὸ καινὸν τοῦ παλαιοῦ, καὶ χεῖρον σχίσμα γίνεται.

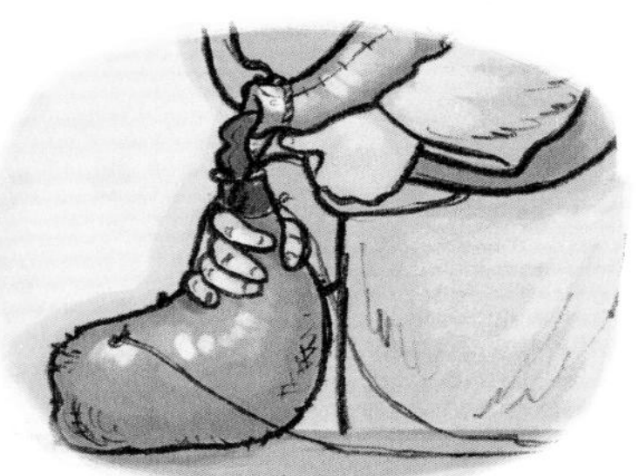

22 καὶ οὐδεὶς βάλλει οἶνον νέον εἰς ἀσκοὺς παλαιούς· εἰ δὲ μή, ῥήξει ὁ οἶνος τοὺς ἀσκούς, καὶ ὁ οἶνος ἀπόλλυται καὶ οἱ ἀσκοί.

ἀλλὰ οἶνον νέον εἰς ἀσκοὺς καινούς.

[17] And after hearing, Jesus says to them this: "The ones being strong have no need of a doctor, but rather the ones having it badly. I did not come to call the righteous, but the sinners!" [18] And John's disciples and the Pharisees were fasting. And they come and say to him, "For what reason do the disciples of John and the disciples of the Pharisees fast, but the your disciples do not fast?" [19] And Jesus said to them, "The sons of the wedding hall, where the groom is with them, aren't able to fast, are they? *No.* For as much time as they have the groom with them, they are not able to fast." [20] "But days will come, whenever the groom is taken away from them, and then they will fast in that very day. [21] "No one sews a piece of undressed cloth upon an old outer garment; but if otherwise, it lifts the fuller part away from it—the new from the old—and becomes a worse tear. [22] "And no one throws new wine into old wineskins; but if otherwise, the wine will break the skins, both the wine is ruined and the skins. However, new wine *is put* into new skins.

23 Καὶ ἐγένετο αὐτὸν ἐν τοῖς σάββασιν παραπορεύεσθαι διὰ τῶν σπορίμων, καὶ οἱ μαθηταὶ αὐτοῦ ἤρξαντο ὁδὸν ποιεῖν τίλλοντες τοὺς στάχυας.
24 καὶ οἱ Φαρισαῖοι ἔλεγον αὐτῷ·
Ἴδε τί ποιοῦσιν τοῖς σάββασιν ὃ οὐκ ἔξεστιν;

25 καὶ λέγει αὐτοῖς·
Οὐδέποτε ἀνέγνωτε τί ἐποίησεν Δαυὶδ ὅτε χρείαν ἔσχεν καὶ ἐπείνασεν αὐτὸς καὶ οἱ μετ᾽ αὐτοῦ; 26 πῶς εἰσῆλθεν εἰς τὸν οἶκον τοῦ θεοῦ ἐπὶ Ἀβιαθὰρ ἀρχιερέως καὶ τοὺς ἄρτους τῆς προθέσεως ἔφαγεν, οὓς οὐκ ἔξεστιν φαγεῖν εἰ μὴ τοὺς ἱερεῖς, καὶ ἔδωκεν καὶ τοῖς σὺν αὐτῷ οὖσιν;
27 καὶ ἔλεγεν αὐτοῖς·
Τὸ σάββατον διὰ τὸν ἄνθρωπον ἐγένετο καὶ οὐχ ὁ ἄνθρωπος διὰ τὸ σάββατον·
28 ὥστε κύριός ἐστιν ὁ υἱὸς τοῦ ἀνθρώπου καὶ τοῦ σαββάτου.

Κεφ. Γ´

1 Καὶ εἰσῆλθεν πάλιν εἰς συναγωγήν, καὶ ἦν ἐκεῖ ἄνθρωπος ἐξηραμμένην ἔχων τὴν χεῖρα. 2 καὶ παρετήρουν αὐτὸν εἰ τοῖς σάββασιν θεραπεύσει αὐτόν, ἵνα κατηγορήσωσιν αὐτοῦ. 3 καὶ λέγει τῷ ἀνθρώπῳ τῷ τὴν χεῖρα ἔχοντι ξηράν·

Ἔγειρε εἰς τὸ μέσον.
4 καὶ λέγει αὐτοῖς·
Ἔξεστιν τοῖς σάββασιν ἀγαθοποιῆσαι ἢ κακοποιῆσαι, ψυχὴν σῶσαι ἢ ἀποκτεῖναι;
οἱ δὲ ἐσιώπων.

23 And it happened that on the Sabbath Days he was passing along through the grain fields, and his disciples began to make a way while picking the stalks. 24 And the Pharisees were saying to him, "Look, why are they doing on the Sabbath days that which is not allowed?" 25 And he says to them, "Haven't you ever read what David did when
he had a need and was hungry, he and those who were with him? *Surely, yes!* 26 How he entered into the house of God at the time of Abiathar, later high priest, and ate the
loaves of the showbread, which is not allowed to eat except for the priests, and he give *it* also to the ones who were with him?" 27 And he proceeded saying to them: "The
Sabbath was made for humanity, and not humanity for the Sabbath." 28 As a result, then, the Son of Man is Lord even of the Sabbath. 3:1 And he entered again into a synagogue, and there was a person there having a completely withered up hand. 2 And they began monitoring him *to see* if on the Sabbath Days he would heal him, in order
that they would accuse him. 3 And he says to the person having the withered hand, "Rise up into the middle." 4 And he says to them, "Is it allowed on the Sabbath days to
do good or to do harm, to save a life or to kill?" Well, they were keeping quiet.

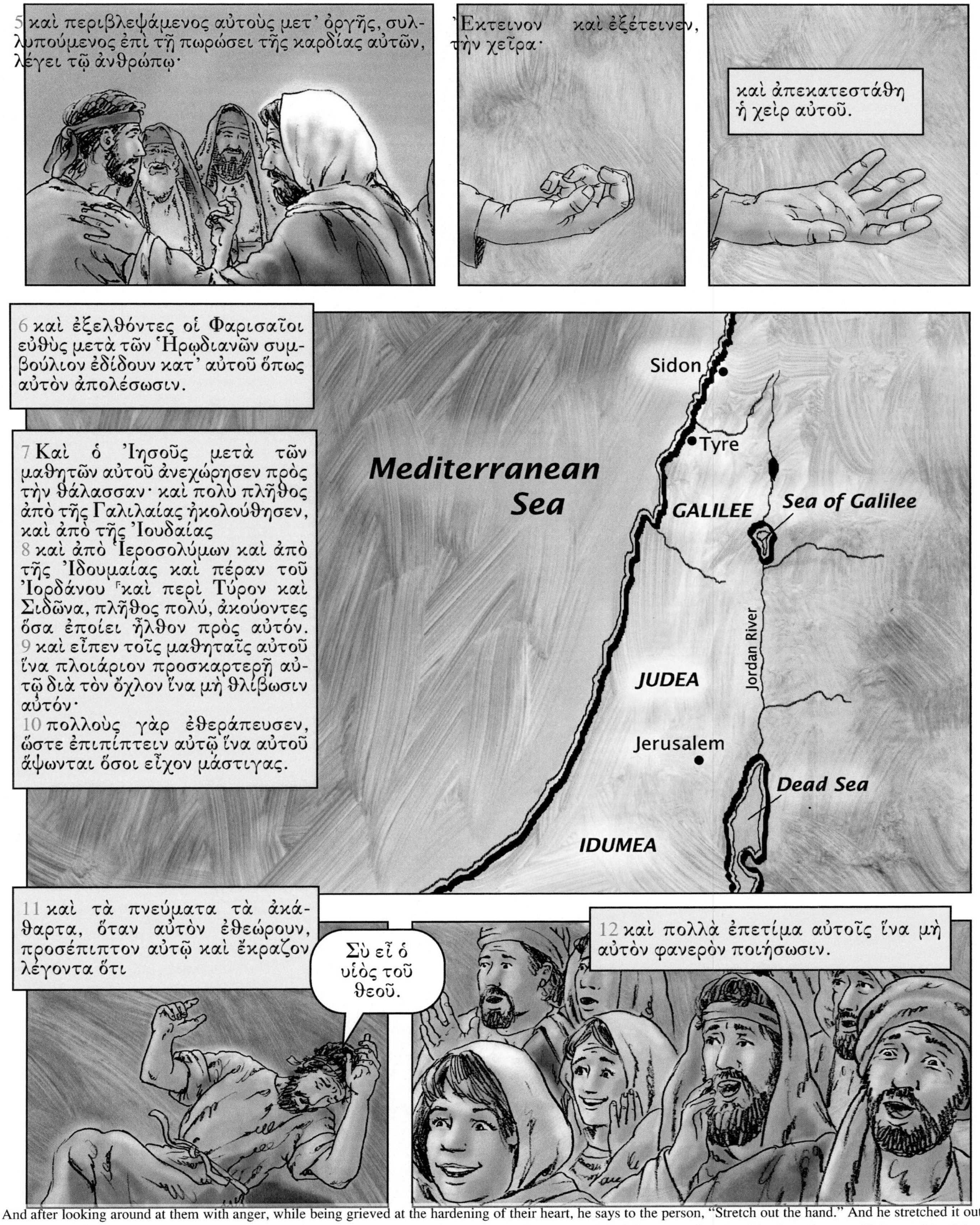

5 καὶ περιβλεψάμενος αὐτοὺς μετ᾽ ὀργῆς, συλ-
λυπούμενος ἐπὶ τῇ πωρώσει τῆς καρδίας αὐτῶν,
λέγει τῷ ἀνθρώπῳ·

Ἔκτεινον
τὴν χεῖρα·
καὶ ἐξέτεινεν,

καὶ ἀπεκατεστάθη
ἡ χεὶρ αὐτοῦ.

6 καὶ ἐξελθόντες οἱ Φαρισαῖοι
εὐθὺς μετὰ τῶν Ἡρῳδιανῶν συμβούλιον ἐδίδουν κατ᾽ αὐτοῦ ὅπως
αὐτὸν ἀπολέσωσιν.

7 Καὶ ὁ Ἰησοῦς μετὰ τῶν
μαθητῶν αὐτοῦ ἀνεχώρησεν πρὸς
τὴν θάλασσαν· καὶ πολὺ πλῆθος
ἀπὸ τῆς Γαλιλαίας ἠκολούθησεν,
καὶ ἀπὸ τῆς Ἰουδαίας
8 καὶ ἀπὸ Ἱεροσολύμων καὶ ἀπὸ
τῆς Ἰδουμαίας καὶ πέραν τοῦ
Ἰορδάνου ⸀καὶ περὶ Τύρον καὶ
Σιδῶνα, πλῆθος πολύ, ἀκούοντες
ὅσα ἐποίει ἦλθον πρὸς αὐτόν.
9 καὶ εἶπεν τοῖς μαθηταῖς αὐτοῦ
ἵνα πλοιάριον προσκαρτερῇ αὐτῷ διὰ τὸν ὄχλον ἵνα μὴ θλίβωσιν
αὐτόν·
10 πολλοὺς γὰρ ἐθεράπευσεν,
ὥστε ἐπιπίπτειν αὐτῷ ἵνα αὐτοῦ
ἅψωνται ὅσοι εἶχον μάστιγας.

Sidon
Tyre
Mediterranean Sea
GALILEE
Sea of Galilee
Jordan River
JUDEA
Jerusalem
Dead Sea
IDUMEA

11 καὶ τὰ πνεύματα τὰ ἀκάθαρτα, ὅταν αὐτὸν ἐθεώρουν,
προσέπιπτον αὐτῷ καὶ ἔκραζον
λέγοντα ὅτι

Σὺ εἶ ὁ υἱὸς τοῦ θεοῦ.

12 καὶ πολλὰ ἐπετίμα αὐτοῖς ἵνα μὴ
αὐτὸν φανερὸν ποιήσωσιν.

5 And after looking around at them with anger, while being grieved at the hardening of their heart, he says to the person, "Stretch out the hand." And he stretched it out, and his hand was restored. 6 And after going out, the Pharisees straightaway with the Herodians proceeded giving counsel against him, how they would destroy him. 7 And Jesus with his disciples withdrew to the sea; and a great multitude from Galilee followed; and from Judaea 8 and from Jerusalem and from Idumaea and beyond the Jordan and around Tyre and Sidon, a great multitude, after hearing how much he was doing, came to him. 9 And he spoke to his disciples in order that they would prepare a boat for him because of the crowd, lest they should crush him; 10 for he healed many, so that they were falling before him, in order that they would touch him, as many as were having afflictions. 11 And the unclean spirits, whenever they were seeing him, were falling down before him and were crying out saying this: "You yourself are the Son of God!" 12 And many times he was rebuking them, in order that they would not make him known.

13 Καὶ ἀναβαίνει εἰς τὸ ὄρος καὶ
προσκαλεῖται οὓς ἤθελεν αὐτός,
καὶ ἀπῆλθον πρὸς αὐτόν.
14 καὶ ἐποίησεν δώδεκα, ἵνα ὦσιν
μετ᾽ αὐτοῦ καὶ ἵνα ἀποστέλλῃ
αὐτοὺς κηρύσσειν
15 καὶ ἔχειν ἐξουσίαν ἐκβάλλειν
τὰ δαιμόνια·

16 καὶ ἐποίησεν τοὺς δώδεκα, καὶ
ἐπέθηκεν ὄνομα τῷ Σίμωνι Πέτρον,
17 καὶ Ἰάκωβον τὸν τοῦ Ζεβεδαίου καὶ Ἰωάννην τὸν ἀδελφὸν
τοῦ Ἰακώβου (καὶ ἐπέθηκεν
αὐτοῖς ὀνόματα Βοανηργές, ὅ
ἐστιν Υἱοὶ Βροντῆς),

18 καὶ Ἀνδρέαν καὶ Φίλιππον
καὶ Βαρθολομαῖον καὶ Μαθ-
θαῖον καὶ Θωμᾶν καὶ Ἰάκωβον
τὸν τοῦ Ἀλφαίου καὶ Θαδδαῖον
καὶ Σίμωνα τὸν Καναναῖον
19 καὶ Ἰούδαν Ἰσκαριώθ, ὃς καὶ
παρέδωκεν αὐτόν.

20 Καὶ ἔρχεται εἰς οἶκον·
καὶ συνέρχεται πάλιν ὁ
ὄχλος, ὥστε μὴ δύνασθαι
αὐτοὺς μηδὲ ἄρτον φα-
γεῖν.
21 καὶ ἀκούσαντες οἱ παρ᾽
αὐτοῦ ἐξῆλθον κρατῆσαι
αὐτόν, ἔλεγον γὰρ ὅτι
ἐξέστη.

[13] And he goes up into the mountain and calls those whom he himself was wanting, and they went to him. [14] And he appointed twelve, in order that they would be with
him and in order that he would send them out to be preaching [15] and to be having authority to be casting out the demons. [16] And he appointed the twelve, and he placed
upon Simon the name Peter, [17] and Jacob, the *son* of Zebedee, and John, the brother of Jacob, he even placed upon them the name Boanerges, that is "Sons of Thunder,"
[18] and Andrew and Philip and Bartholomew and Matthew and Thomas and Jacob, the *son* of Alphaeus, and Thaddaeus and Simon, the Canaanite, [19] and Judas Iscariot,
who also handed him over. [20] And he comes into a house; and the crowd again begins gathering together, so that they could not even eat bread. [21] And after hearing, those
with him went out to take hold of him, for they were saying that he had lost his senses.

22 καὶ οἱ γραμματεῖς οἱ ἀπὸ Ἱεροσολύμων καταβάντες ἔλεγον ὅτι

Βεελζεβοὺλ ἔχει.

καὶ ὅτι

ἐν τῷ ἄρχοντι τῶν δαιμονίων ἐκβάλλει τὰ δαιμόνια.

23 καὶ προσκαλεσάμενος αὐτοὺς ἐν παραβολαῖς ἔλεγεν αὐτοῖς·

πῶς δύναται Σατανᾶς Σατανᾶν ἐκβάλλειν;
24 καὶ ἐὰν βασιλεία ἐφ' ἑαυτὴν μερισθῇ, οὐ δύναται σταθῆναι ἡ βασιλεία ἐκείνη·
25 καὶ ἐὰν οἰκία ἐφ' ἑαυτὴν μερισθῇ, οὐ δυνήσεται ἡ οἰκία ἐκείνη σταθῆναι·
26 καὶ εἰ ὁ Σατανᾶς ἀνέστη ἐφ' ἑαυτὸν καὶ ἐμερίσθη, οὐ δύναται στῆναι ἀλλὰ τέλος ἔχει.
27 ἀλλ' οὐδεὶς δύναται εἰς τὴν οἰκίαν τοῦ ἰσχυροῦ εἰσελθὼν τὰ σκεύη αὐτοῦ διαρπάσαι ἐὰν μὴ πρῶτον τὸν ἰσχυρὸν δήσῃ, καὶ τότε τὴν οἰκίαν αὐτοῦ διαρπάσει.
28 Ἀμὴν λέγω ὑμῖν ὅτι πάντα ἀφεθήσεται τοῖς υἱοῖς τῶν ἀνθρώπων, τὰ ἁμαρτήματα καὶ αἱ βλασφημίαι ὅσα ἐὰν βλασφημήσωσιν·
29 ὃς δ' ἂν βλασφημήσῃ εἰς τὸ πνεῦμα τὸ ἅγιον, οὐκ ἔχει ἄφεσιν εἰς τὸν αἰῶνα, ἀλλὰ ἔνοχός ἐστιν αἰωνίου ἁμαρτήματος.

30 ὅτι ἔλεγον· Πνεῦμα ἀκάθαρτον ἔχει.

31 Καὶ ἔρχονται ἡ μήτηρ αὐτοῦ καὶ οἱ ἀδελφοὶ αὐτοῦ καὶ ἔξω στήκοντες ἀπέστειλαν πρὸς αὐτὸν καλοῦντες αὐτόν.
32 καὶ ἐκάθητο περὶ αὐτὸν ὄχλος, καὶ λέγουσιν αὐτῷ·
Ἰδοὺ ἡ μήτηρ σου καὶ οἱ ἀδελφοί σου ἔξω ζητοῦσίν σε.
33 καὶ ἀποκριθεὶς αὐτοῖς λέγει·
Τίς ἐστιν ἡ μήτηρ μου ἢ οἱ ἀδελφοί μου;

[22] And the scribes coming down from Jerusalem were saying this: “He has Beelzebub,” and this: “By the prince of the demons he is casting out the demons.” [23] And after
calling to them, he was speaking to them in parables: “How is Satan able to be casting out Satan? [24] And if ever a kingdom is divided against itself, that kingdom is not
able to stand. [25] And if a house is divided against itself, that house is not able to stand. [26] And if Satan stood up against himself and was divided, he is not able to stand but
has an end. [27] But no one is able, after entering into the house of a strong man, to plunder his belongings unless first he binds the strong man, and then he will loot his
house. [28] Amen! I am saying to you that all things will be forgiven the sons of people, the sins and the blasphemies however much they blaspheme; [29] but whoever
blasphemes against the Holy Spirit does not have forgiveness into the age, but is guilty of an eternal sin.” [30] because they were saying, “He has an unclean spirit.” [31] And
his mother and his brothers come and, while standing outside, they sent for him, calling him. [32] And a crowd was sitting around him and they say to him, “Behold, your
mother and your brothers are outside seeking you.” [33] And answering back to them, he says, “Who is my mother or my brothers?”

34 καὶ περιβλεψάμενος τοὺς περὶ
αὐτὸν κύκλῳ καθημένους λέγει·
Ἴδε ἡ μήτηρ
μου καὶ οἱ ἀδελφοί
μου·
35 ὃς γὰρ ἂν ποιήσῃ
τὸ θέλημα τοῦ θεοῦ,
οὗτος ἀδελφός μου
καὶ ἀδελφὴ καὶ
μήτηρ ἐστίν.

Κεφ.
Δ´

1 Καὶ πάλιν ἤρξατο διδά-
σκειν παρὰ τὴν θάλασσαν.
καὶ συνάγεται πρὸς αὐτὸν
ὄχλος πλεῖστος, ὥστε αὐτὸν
εἰς πλοῖον ἐμβάντα καθῆ-
σθαι ἐν τῇ θαλάσσῃ, καὶ πᾶς
ὁ ὄχλος πρὸς τὴν θάλασσαν
ἐπὶ τῆς γῆς ἦσαν.
2 καὶ ἐδίδασκεν αὐτοὺς ἐν
παρα-βολαῖς πολλά καὶ
ἔλεγεν αὐτοῖς ἐν τῇ διδαχῇ
αὐτοῦ·

3 Ἀκούετε. ἰδοὺ ἐξῆλθεν ὁ
σπείρων σπεῖραι.

4 καὶ ἐγένετο ἐν τῷ σπεί-
ρειν ὃ μὲν ἔπεσεν παρὰ τὴν
ὁδόν, καὶ ἦλθεν τὰ πετεινὰ
καὶ κατέφαγεν αὐτό.
5 καὶ ἄλλο ἔπεσεν ἐπὶ τὸ
πετρῶδες ὅπου οὐκ εἶχεν γῆν

πολλήν, καὶ εὐθὺς ἐξανέτει-λεν
διὰ τὸ μὴ ἔχειν βάθος γῆς·
6 καὶ ὅτε ἀνέτειλεν ὁ ἥλιος

ἐκαυματίσθη καὶ διὰ τὸ μὴ
ἔχειν ῥίζαν ἐξηράνθη.

7 καὶ ἄλλο ἔπεσεν εἰς τὰς ἀκάνθας, καὶ ἀνέβησαν αἱ ἄκανθαι καὶ
συνέπνιξαν αὐτό, καὶ καρπὸν οὐκ
ἔδωκεν.

34 And after looking around at those sitting in a circle around him, he says, “Look, my mother and my brothers! 35 For whoever who does the will of God, this one is my
brother, and a sister, and a mother.” 4:1 And again he began to teach by the seaside. And a very large crowd begins gathering together with him, so that he, after entering
into a boat, sat in the sea, and all the crowd at the sea was on the land. 2 And he proceeded teaching them many things in parables and he was saying to them in his teaching,
3 “Listen. Behold, the one sowing went out to sow. 4 And it happened in the sowing that some fell beside the path, and the birds came and ate it. 5 And other *seed* fell upon
the rocky ground where it was not having much soil, and straightaway it sprang up because it was not having depth of soil; 6 and when the sun arose, it was scorched and,
because it didn’t have a root, it withered. 7 And other *seed* fell among the thorns, and the thorns came up and choked it, and it did not give fruit.

8 καὶ [ἄλλο] ἔπεσεν εἰς τὴν γῆν τὴν καλήν, καὶ ἐδίδου καρπὸν ἀναβαίνοντα καὶ αὐξανόμενα, καὶ ἔφερεν ἓν τριάκοντα καὶ ἓν ἑξήκοντα καὶ ἓν ἑκατόν.
9 καὶ ἔλεγεν·
Ὃς ἔχει ὦτα ἀκούειν ἀκουέτω.

10 Καὶ ὅτε ἐγένετο κατὰ μόνας, ἠρώτων αὐτὸν οἱ περὶ αὐτὸν σὺν τοῖς δώδεκα τὰς παραβολάς.
11 καὶ ἔλεγεν αὐτοῖς·

Ὑμῖν τὸ μυστήριον δέδοται τῆς βασιλείας τοῦ θεοῦ· ἐκείνοις δὲ τοῖς ἔξω ἐν παραβολαῖς τὰ πάντα γίνεται,

12 ἵνα βλέποντες βλέπωσι καὶ μὴ ἴδωσιν, καὶ ἀκούοντες ἀκούωσι καὶ μὴ συνιῶσιν, μήποτε ἐπιστρέψωσιν καὶ ἀφεθῇ αὐτοῖς.

13 Καὶ λέγει αὐτοῖς·

Οὐκ οἴδατε τὴν παραβολὴν ταύτην, καὶ πῶς πάσας τὰς παραβολὰς γνώσεσθε;
14 Ὁ σπείρων τὸν λόγον σπείρει.

15 οὗτοι δέ εἰσιν οἱ παρὰ τὴν ὁδὸν ὅπου σπείρεται ὁ λόγος, καὶ ὅταν ἀκούσωσιν εὐθὺς ἔρχεται ὁ Σατανᾶς καὶ αἴρει τὸν λόγον τὸν ἐσπαρμένον εἰς αὐτούς.

16 καὶ οὗτοί εἰσιν ὁμοίως οἱ ἐπὶ τὰ πετρώδη σπειρόμενοι, οἳ ὅταν ἀκούσωσιν τὸν λόγον εὐθὺς μετὰ χαρᾶς λαμβάνουσιν αὐτόν,

17 καὶ οὐκ ἔχουσιν ῥίζαν ἐν ἑαυτοῖς ἀλλὰ πρόσκαιροί εἰσιν,

εἶτα γενομένης θλίψεως ἢ διωγμοῦ διὰ τὸν λόγον εὐθὺς σκανδαλίζονται.
18 καὶ ἄλλοι εἰσὶν οἱ εἰς τὰς ἀκάνθας σπειρόμενοι· οὗτοί εἰσιν οἱ τὸν λόγον ἀκούσαντες,
19 καὶ αἱ μέριμναι τοῦ αἰῶνος καὶ ἡ ἀπάτη τοῦ πλούτου καὶ αἱ περὶ τὰ λοιπὰ ἐπιθυμίαι εἰσπορευόμεναι συμπνίγουσιν τὸν λόγον, καὶ ἄκαρπος γίνεται.

8 And others fell into the good ground, and were giving fruit, coming up and growing, and one was bearing thirty, and one sixty, and one a hundred fold." 9 And he was
saying, "The one who has ears to be listening, keep listening!" 10 And when he became alone, the ones around him with the Twelve were asking him about the parables.
11 And he was saying to them, "To you the mystery of the Kingdom of God has been given; but to those outside all things come in parables 12 in order that, although seeing,
they would see and not perceive, and, although hearing, they would hear and not comprehend, otherwise they would turn and it would be forgiven them." 13 And he says
them, "Haven't you understood this parable? *Surely, yes!* How even will you understand all the parables? 14 The one sowing sows the word. 15 Now, these are the ones who
are by the path where the word is being sown, and whenever they hear, straightaway the accuser comes and takes away the word that has been sown into them. 16 And
these ones are like those seeds being sown upon the rocky path, which whenever they hear the word, straightaway with joy they receive it, 17 and they are not having root
in themselves but they are existing only for a short time, then, after trouble or persecution occurs on account of the word, immediately they are caused to stumble. 18 And
others are the ones being sown into the thorns; these are the ones hearing the word, 19 and the worries of this age and the deceitfulness of riches and the desires concerning
the remaining things, when coming in, choke the word, and it becomes fruitless.

γῆν τὴν καλὴν σπαρέντες, οἵτινες
ἀκούουσιν τὸν λόγον καὶ παραδέ-
χονται καὶ καρποφοροῦσιν ἓν
τριάκοντα καὶ ἓν ἑξήκοντα καὶ ἓν
ἑκατόν.

21 Καὶ ἔλεγεν αὐτοῖς·

Μήτι ἔρχεται ὁ λύχνος ἵνα ὑπὸ τὸν
μόδιον τεθῇ ἢ ὑπὸ τὴν κλίνην, οὐχ
ἵνα ἐπὶ τὴν λυχνίαν τεθῇ;
22 οὐ γάρ ἐστιν κρυπτὸν ἐὰν μὴ ἵνα
φανερωθῇ, οὐδὲ ἐγένετο ἀπόκ-
ρυφον ἀλλ᾽ ἵνα ἔλθῃ εἰς φανερόν.
23 εἴ τις ἔχει ὦτα ἀκούειν ἀκουέτω.
24 καὶ ἔλεγεν αὐτοῖς· Βλέπετε τί
ἀκούετε. ἐν ᾧ μέτρῳ μετρεῖτε με-
ται ὑμῖν.
25 ὃς γὰρ ἔχει, δοθήσεται αὐτῷ·
καὶ ὃς οὐκ ἔχει, καὶ ὃ ἔχει
ἀρθήσεται ἀπ᾽ αὐτοῦ.

26 Καὶ ἔλεγεν·

Οὕτως ἐστὶν ἡ βασιλεία τοῦ θεοῦ
ὡς ἄνθρωπος βάλῃ τὸν σπόρον ἐπὶ
τῆς γῆς
27 καὶ καθεύδῃ καὶ ἐγείρηται
νύκτα καὶ ἡμέραν, καὶ ὁ σπόρος
βλαστᾷ καὶ μηκύνηται ὡς οὐκ
οἶδεν αὐτός.
28 αὐτομάτη ἡ γῆ καρποφορεῖ,
πρῶτον χόρτον, εἶτα στάχυν, εἶτα
πλήρης σῖτον ἐν τῷ στάχυϊ.
29 ὅταν δὲ παραδοῖ ὁ καρπός,
ὅτι παρέστηκεν ὁ θερισμός.

30 Καὶ ἔλεγεν·

Πῶς ὁμοιώσωμεν τὴν βασιλείαν
τοῦ θεοῦ, ἢ ἐν τίνι αὐτὴν
παραβολῇ θῶμεν;
31 ὡς κόκκῳ σινάπεως, ὃς ὅταν
σπαρῇ ἐπὶ τῆς γῆς, μικρότερον ὂν
πάντων τῶν σπερμάτων τῶν ἐπὶ
τῆς γῆς—
32 καὶ ὅταν σπαρῇ, ἀναβαίνει καὶ
γίνεται μεῖζον πάντων τῶν λαχά-
νων καὶ ποιεῖ κλάδους μεγάλους,
ὥστε δύνασθαι ὑπὸ τὴν σκιὰν
αὐτοῦ τὰ πετεινὰ τοῦ οὐρανοῦ
κατασκηνοῦν.

33 Καὶ τοιαύταις παραβολαῖς
πολλαῖς ἐλάλει αὐτοῖς τὸν
λόγον, καθὼς ἠδύναντο ἀκούειν·
34 χωρὶς δὲ παραβολῆς οὐκ
ἐλάλει αὐτοῖς, κατ᾽ ἰδίαν δὲ
τοῖς ἰδίοις μαθηταῖς ἐπέλυεν
πάντα.

[20] And those are the ones sown upon the good ground, who are hearing the word and are receiving *it* and are bearing fruit—one thirty, and one sixty, and one a hundred fold." [21] And he was saying to them, "The lamp doesn't come out, does it, in order that it would placed under the basket or under the couch? *Surely, not! Is it not rather brought out* in order that it would be placed on the lamp stand? *Surely, yes!* [22] For it is not hidden, unless in order that it would be made plainly visible; moreover, neither did it become a secret, but in order that it would come into plain sight. [23] If anyone has ears to be listening, keep listening!" [24] And he was saying to them, "Be aware what you are listening to: By which measure you are measuring, it will be measured to you and accounted to you. [25] For the one who has, it will be given to him; and the one who does not have, even what he has will be taken from him." [26] And he was saying, "Thus the kingdom of God is like a man who throws the seed on the ground [27] and sleeps and rises up, night and day, and the seed sprouts and grows; how, he himself does not know. [28] Automatically the ground bears fruit: first grass, then a stalk, then a full grain in the stalk. [29] Additionally, whenever the fruit produces, straightaway he sends for the sickle because the harvest has come near." [30] And he was saying, "How should we compare the Kingdom of God, or in what parable should we place it? [31] Like a grain of mustard, which, whenever it is scattered on the ground, being smaller than all of the seeds on the ground, [32] and whenever it is scattered, it comes up and becomes greater than all the garden-herbs and makes wide branches, so that the birds of the sky are able to dwell under its shade." [33] And with many parables such as these he was speaking to them the word, just as they were able to listen; [34] but without a parable he was not speaking to them, but in private to his own disciples he was explaining everything.

35 Καὶ λέγει αὐτοῖς ἐν ἐκείνῃ τῇ ἡμέρᾳ ὀψίας γενομένης·
Διέλθωμεν εἰς τὸ πέραν.
36 καὶ ἀφέντες τὸν ὄχλον παραλαμβάνουσιν αὐτὸν ὡς ἦν ἐν τῷ πλοίῳ, καὶ ἄλλα πλοῖα ἦν μετ᾽ αὐτοῦ.
37 καὶ γίνεται λαῖλαψ μεγάλη ἀνέμου, καὶ τὰ κύματα ἐπέβαλλεν εἰς τὸ πλοῖον, ὥστε ἤδη γεμίζεσθαι τὸ πλοῖον.

38 καὶ αὐτὸς ἦν ἐν τῇ πρύμνῃ ἐπὶ τὸ προσκεφάλαιον καθεύδων· καὶ ἐγείρουσιν αὐτὸν καὶ λέγουσιν αὐτῷ·

Διδάσκαλε, οὐ μέλει σοι ὅτι ἀπολλύμεθα;

39 καὶ διεγερθεὶς

ἐπετίμησεν τῷ ἀνέμῳ καὶ εἶπεν τῇ θαλάσσῃ·

Σιώπα, πεφίμωσο.

[35] And he says to them on that *very* day when evening came, "Let us cross to the other side." [36] And after leaving the crowd, they took him along as he was in the boat and other boats were with him. [37] And a great gust of a wind arises and was throwing the waves into the boat, so that already the boat was being filled up. [38] And he himself was in the stern on the pillow sleeping. And they wake him up and say to him, "Teacher, Doesn't it concern you that we are perishing? *Surely, yes!*" [39] And after awakened, he rebuked the wind and he said to the sea, "Be quiet, be silent!" And the wind stopped, and there came a great calm.

ὁ ἄνεμος, καὶ ἐγένετο γα-λήνη μεγάλη.

Τί δειλοί ἐστε; οὔπω ἔχετε πίστιν;

καὶ ἔλεγον πρὸς ἀλλήλους·
Τίς ἄρα οὗτός ἐστιν ὅτι καὶ ὁ ἄνεμος καὶ ἡ θάλασσα ὑπακούει αὐτῷ;

Κεφ.
Ε´

1 Καὶ ἦλθον εἰς τὸ πέραν τῆς θαλάσσης εἰς τὴν χώραν τῶν Γερασηνῶν.
2 καὶ ἐξελθόντος αὐτοῦ ἐκ τοῦ
πλοίου εὐθὺς ὑπήντησεν αὐτῷ ἐκ
τῶν μνημείων ἄνθρωπος ἐν πνεύματι
ἀκαθάρτῳ,
3 ὃς τὴν κατοίκησιν εἶχεν ἐν τοῖς
μνήμασιν, καὶ οὐδὲ ἁλύσει οὐκέτι
οὐδεὶς ἐδύνατο αὐτὸν δῆσαι
4 διὰ τὸ αὐτὸν πολλάκις πέδαις καὶ
ἁλύσεσι δεδέσθαι καὶ διεσπάσθαι
ὑπ᾽ αὐτοῦ τὰς ἁλύσεις καὶ τὰς πέδας
συντετρῖφθαι, καὶ οὐδεὶς ἴσχυεν
αὐτὸν δαμάσαι·

5 καὶ διὰ παντὸς νυκτὸς καὶ ἡμέρας ἐν τοῖς μνήμασιν καὶ ἐν τοῖς ὄρεσιν ἦν κρά-ζων καὶ κατακόπτων ἑαυτὸν λίθοις.
6 καὶ ἰδὼν τὸν Ἰησοῦν ἀπὸ μακρόθεν ἔδραμεν καὶ προσεκύνησεν αὐτόν,
7 καὶ κράξας φωνῇ μεγάλῃ λέγει·
Τί ἐμοὶ καὶ σοί, Ἰησοῦ υἱὲ τοῦ θεοῦ τοῦ ὑψίστου; ὁρκίζω σε τὸν θεόν, μή με βασανίσῃς.
8 ἔλεγεν γὰρ αὐτῷ·
Ἔξελθε τὸ πνεῦμα τὸ ἀκάθαρτον ἐκ τοῦ ἀνθρώπου.

9 καὶ ἐπηρώτα αὐτόν·
Τί ὄνομά σοι;
καὶ λέγει αὐτῷ·
Λεγιὼν ὄνομά μοι, ὅτι πολλοί ἐσμεν·
10 καὶ παρεκάλει αὐτὸν πολλὰ ἵνα μὴ αὐτὰ ἀποστείλῃ ἔξω τῆς χώρας.
11 ἦν δὲ ἐκεῖ πρὸς τῷ ὄρει ἀγέλη χοίρων μεγάλη βοσκομένη·

40 And he said to them, "Why are you cowardly? Don't you yet have faith? *Surely, Yes!*" 41 And they were afraid, very afraid, and they were saying to one another, "Who
then is this, because both the wind and the sea obey him?" 5:1 And they went to the other side of the sea into the region of the Gerasenes. 2 And after he came out from
the boat, straightaway there met him from out of the tombs a person with an unclean spirit, 3 who was having his home in the tombs, and not even with a chain any longer
was anyone able to bind him 4 because he, many times with shackles and chains, had been bound, and the chains had been torn apart by him, and the shackles had been
crushed; and no one was being strong enough to subdue him. 5 And throughout every night and day in the tombs and on the mountains, he was crying out and cutting
himself with stones. 6 And after seeing Jesus from afar, he ran and fell down prostrate before him, 7 and, after crying out in a loud voice, he says, "What do our affairs *have
to do* with yours, Jesus, Son of the God Most High? I am imploring you before God, do not torture me!" 8 For he was saying to him, "Come out, unclean spirit, from the
person!" 9 And he was asking him, "What is your name?" And he says to him, "Legion is my name, because we are many " 10 And he was imploring him a lot, in order
that he would not be sent outside of the region. 11 Now there at the mountain was a large herd of pigs feeding.

κα παρεκ εσαν
αὐτὸν λέγοντες·
Πέμψον ἡμᾶς εἰς τοὺς χοίρους, ἵνα εἰς αὐτοὺς εἰσέλθωμεν.

τὰ πνεύματα τὰ ἀκάθαρτα εἰσῆλθον εἰς τοὺς χοίρους, καὶ ὥρμησεν ἡ ἀγέλη κατὰ τοῦ κρημνοῦ εἰς τὴν θάλασσαν, ὡς δισχίλιοι, καὶ ἐπνίγοντο ἐν τῇ θαλάσσῃ.

14 Καὶ οἱ βόσκοντες αὐτοὺς ἔφυγον καὶ ἀπήγγειλαν εἰς τὴν πόλιν καὶ εἰς τοὺς ἀγρούς· καὶ ἦλθον ἰδεῖν τί ἐστιν τὸ γεγονός.
15 καὶ ἔρχονται πρὸς τὸν Ἰησοῦν, καὶ θεωροῦσιν τὸν δαιμονιζόμενον καθήμενον ἱματισμένον καὶ σωφρονοῦντα, τὸν ἐσχηκότα τὸν λεγιῶνα, καὶ ἐφοβήθησαν.

16 καὶ διηγήσαντο αὐτοῖς οἱ ἰδόντες πῶς ἐγένετο τῷ δαιμονιζομένῳ καὶ περὶ τῶν χοίρων.
17 καὶ ἤρξαντο παρακαλεῖν αὐτὸν ἀπελθεῖν ἀπὸ τῶν ὁρίων αὐτῶν.

18 καὶ ἐμβαίνοντος αὐτοῦ εἰς τὸ πλοῖον παρεκάλει αὐτὸν ὁ δαιμονισθεὶς ἵνα μετ᾽ αὐτοῦ ᾖ.

19 καὶ οὐκ ἀφῆκεν αὐτόν, ἀλλὰ λέγει αὐτῷ·

Ὕπαγε εἰς τὸν οἶκόν σου πρὸς τοὺς σούς, καὶ ἀπάγγειλον αὐτοῖς ὅσα ὁ κύριός σοι πεποίηκεν καὶ ἠλέησέν σε.

20 καὶ ἀπῆλθεν καὶ ἤρξατο κηρύσσειν ἐν τῇ Δεκαπόλει ὅσα ἐποίησεν αὐτῷ ὁ Ἰησοῦς, καὶ πάντες ἐθαύμαζον.

21 Καὶ διαπεράσαντος τοῦ Ἰησοῦ ἐν τῷ πλοίῳ πάλιν εἰς τὸ πέραν συνήχθη ὄχλος πολὺς ἐπ᾽ αὐτόν, καὶ ἦν παρὰ τὴν θάλασσαν.

12 And they also begged him saying, “Send us into the pigs, in order that we would enter into them.” 13 And he permitted them. And after going out, the unclean spirits
entered into the pigs, and the herd rushed down the bank into the sea, about two thousand, and they were drowning in the sea. 14 And the ones feeding them fled and
brought a report into the city and into the fields. And they came to see what it was that had happened. 15 And they come to Jesus, and they observe the demon-possessed
person sitting, having been dressed and thinking clearly—the one who had had the legion—and they became afraid. 16 And the ones who had seen reported to them how
it happened to the demon-possessed man and concerning the pigs. 17 And they began to implore him to depart from their regions. 18 And while he was entering the boat,
the man having been demon-possessed was imploring him that he would be with him. 19 And he did not permit him, but he tells him, “Go into your house to those belonging
to you, and report to them how much the Lord has done for you and showed mercy to you.” 20 And he departed and began to proclaim in Decapolis how much Jesus had
done for him, and they all were marveling. 21 And after Jesus crossed over in the boat, again on the other side a large crowd gathered to him, and he was by the sea.

καὶ ἔρχεται εἷς τῶν
ἀρχισυναγώγων, ὀνόματι
Ἰάϊρος, καὶ ἰδὼν αὐτὸν πί-
πτει πρὸς τοὺς πόδας
αὐτοῦ
καὶ παρακαλεῖ αὐτὸν
πολλὰ λέγων ὅτι
Τὸ θυγάτριόν μου ἐσ-
χάτως ἔχει, ἵνα ἐλθὼν ἐπι-
θῇς τὰς χεῖρας αὐτῇ ἵνα
σωθῇ καὶ ζήσῃ.

24 καὶ ἀπῆλθεν μετ' αὐτοῦ. Καὶ ἠκολούθει αὐτῷ ὄχλος πολύς, καὶ συνέθλιβον
αὐτόν.
25 καὶ γυνὴ οὖσα ἐν ῥύσει αἵματος δώδεκα ἔτη
26 καὶ πολλὰ παθοῦσα ὑπὸ πολλῶν
ἰατρῶν

καὶ δαπανήσασα τὰ παρ' αὐτῆς
πάντα καὶ μηδὲν ὠφεληθεῖσα
ἀλλὰ μᾶλλον εἰς τὸ χεῖρον ἐλθοῦσα, .
27 ἀκούσασα περὶ τοῦ Ἰησοῦ,
ἐλθοῦσα ἐν τῷ ὄχλῳ ὄπισθεν
ἥψατο τοῦ ἱματίου αὐτοῦ·
28 ἔλεγεν γὰρ ὅτι

Ἐὰν ἅψωμαι κἂν τῶν ἱματίων
αὐτοῦ σωθήσομαι.

29 καὶ εὐθὺς ἐξηράνθη ἡ
πηγὴ τοῦ αἵματος αὐτῆς,
καὶ ἔγνω τῷ σώματι ὅτι
ἴαται ἀπὸ τῆς μάστιγος.
30 καὶ εὐθὺς ὁ Ἰησοῦς
ἐπιγνοὺς ἐν ἑαυτῷ τὴν ἐξ
αὐτοῦ δύναμιν ἐξελθοῦ-
σαν

22 And there comes one of the synagogue officials, named Jairus, and, after seeing him, he falls before his feet 23 and implores him many things, saying this: "My daughter
is at her end; so that, after coming, you would place your hands upon her in order that she would be restored and live." 24 And he departed with him. And a great crowd
was following him and pressing in on him. 25 And a woman, being with a flow of blood for twelve years, 26 and having suffered many things by many physicians and
having spent everything belonging to her, and having benefitted nothing but rather to a greater degree having come worse, 27 after hearing about Jesus, after coming come
in the crowd from behind, she touched his clothing. 28 For she was saying this: "If I touch even his clothes, I would be restored." 29 And straightaway the flow of her blood
dried up, and she knew in body that she had been healed from the affliction. 30 And straightaway Jesus, after knowing in himself that the power had gone out from him,
turning in the crowd, was saying: "Who touched my clothes?"

ἐπιστραφεὶς ἐν τῷ ὄχλῳ ἔλεγεν·
Τίς μου ἥψατο τῶν ἱματίων;
31 καὶ ἔλεγον αὐτῷ οἱ μαθηταὶ αὐτοῦ·
Βλέπεις τὸν ὄχλον συνθλίβοντά σε, καὶ λέγεις· Τίς μου ἥψατο;
32 καὶ περιεβλέπετο ἰδεῖν τὴν τοῦτο ποιήσασαν.
33 ἡ δὲ γυνὴ φοβηθεῖσα καὶ τρέμουσα, εἰδυῖα ὃ γέγονεν αὐτῇ, ἦλθεν καὶ προσέπεσεν αὐτῷ καὶ εἶπεν αὐτῷ πᾶσαν τὴν ἀλήθειαν.
34 ὁ δὲ εἶπεν αὐτῇ·

Θυγάτηρ, ἡ πίστις σου σέσωκέν σε· ὕπαγε εἰς εἰρήνην, καὶ ἴσθι ὑγιὴς ἀπὸ τῆς μάστιγός σου.
35 Ἔτι αὐτοῦ λαλοῦντος ἔρχονται ἀπὸ τοῦ ἀρχισυναγώγου λέγοντες ὅτι
Ἡ θυγάτηρ σου ἀπέθανεν· τί ἔτι σκύλλεις τὸν διδάσκαλον;

36 ὁ δὲ Ἰησοῦς παρακούσας τὸν λόγον λαλούμενον λέγει τῷ ἀρχισυναγώγῳ·
Μὴ φοβοῦ, μόνον πίστευε.

37 καὶ οὐκ ἀφῆκεν οὐδένα μετ’ αὐτοῦ συνακολουθῆσαι εἰ μὴ τὸν Πέτρον καὶ Ἰάκωβον καὶ Ἰωάννην τὸν ἀδελφὸν Ἰακώβου.
38 καὶ ἔρχονται εἰς τὸν οἶκον τοῦ ἀρχισυναγώγου, καὶ θεωρεῖ θόρυβον καὶ κλαίοντας καὶ ἀλαλάζοντας πολλά,

39 καὶ εἰσελθὼν λέγει αὐτοῖς·
Τί θορυβεῖσθε καὶ κλαίετε; τὸ παιδίον οὐκ ἀπέθανεν ἀλλὰ καθεύδει.
40 καὶ κατεγέλων αὐτοῦ.

31 And his disciples were saying to him, "You see the crowd pressing against you, and you are saying, 'Who touched me?'" 32 And he was looking around to see the
woman who had done this. 33 Well, the woman, fearing and trembling, after knowing what had happened to her, came and fell down before him and told him all the truth.
34 Then, he said to her, "Daughter, your faith has saved you; go in peace, and be healthy from your affliction." 35 While he was still speaking, they come from the synagogue
ruler come, saying this: "Your daughter died; why are you still bothering the teacher?" 36 But Jesus, after overhearing the word being spoken, says to the synagogue ruler,
"Do not fear, only believe!" 37 And he did not permit any one with him to follow, except Peter and James and John, the brother of James. 38 And they go into the house of
the synagogue ruler, and observe an uproar and people weeping and wailing a lot, 39 and, after entering, he says to them, "Why are you making an uproar and crying? The
child did not die but is sleeping." 40 And they were laughing at him. But, after throwing out everyone, he takes along the father of the child and the mother and those with
him, and walks up to where the child was.

α τ ς κ α ν π ντας παρα αμ νει τ ν πατ ρα το παι ου κα
τὴν μητέρα καὶ τοὺς μετ᾽ αὐτοῦ, καὶ εἰσπορεύεται ὅπου ἦν τὸ παιδίον·

41 καὶ κρατήσας τῆς χειρὸς τοῦ παιδίου λέγει αὐτῇ·

Ταλιθα κουμ.

ὅ ἐστιν μεθερμηνευόμενον· Τὸ κοράσιον, σοὶ λέγω, ἔγειρε.

42 καὶ εὐθὺς ἀνέστη τὸ κοράσιον καὶ περιεπάτει, ἦν γὰρ ἐτῶν δώδεκα. καὶ ἐξέστησαν εὐθὺς ἐκστάσει μεγάλῃ.
43 καὶ διεστείλατο αὐτοῖς πολλὰ ἵνα μηδεὶς γνοῖ τοῦτο, καὶ εἶπεν δοθῆναι αὐτῇ φαγεῖν.

Κεφ.
F´

1 Καὶ ἐξῆλθεν ἐκεῖθεν, καὶ ἔρχεται εἰς τὴν πατρίδα αὐτοῦ, καὶ ἀκολουθοῦσιν αὐτῷ οἱ μαθηταὶ αὐτοῦ.
2 καὶ γενομένου σαββάτου ἤρξατο διδάσκειν ἐν τῇ συναγωγῇ· καὶ οἱ πολλοὶ ἀκούοντες ἐξεπλήσσοντο λέγοντες·
Πόθεν τούτῳ ταῦτα, καὶ τίς ἡ σοφία ἡ δοθεῖσα τούτῳ, καὶ αἱ δυνάμεις τοιαῦται διὰ τῶν χειρῶν αὐτοῦ γινόμεναι;

41 And after grasping the hand of the child, he says to her, "'Talitha cum!' which is translated, 'Little girl,' I am saying to you, 'Arise!'" 42 And straightaway the little girl arose and was walking around, for she was twelve years old. And straightaway they were bewildered with great astonishment. 43 And he commanded them many things, in order that nobody should know this, and he said that *something* should be given to her to eat. 6:1 And he went out from there, and goes into his own hometown, and his disciples follow him. 2 And after the Sabbath came, he began to teach in the synagogue; and the many hearing were marveling saying, "From where *do* these things *come* to this man? And what wisdom is given to this man, and such miracles as these being done by his hands?

3 οὐχ οὗτός ἐστιν ὁ τέκτων, ὁ υἱὸς τῆς Μαρίας καὶ ἀδελφὸς Ἰακώβου καὶ Ἰωσῆτος καὶ Ἰούδα καὶ Σίμωνος; καὶ οὐκ εἰσὶν αἱ ἀδελφαὶ αὐτοῦ ὧδε πρὸς ἡμᾶς;

καὶ ἐσκανδαλίζοντο ἐν αὐτῷ.
4 καὶ ἔλεγεν αὐτοῖς ὁ Ἰησοῦς ὅτι

Οὐκ ἔστιν προφήτης ἄτιμος εἰ μὴ ἐν τῇ πατρίδι αὐτοῦ καὶ ἐν τοῖς συγγενεῦσιν αὐτοῦ καὶ ἐν τῇ οἰκίᾳ αὐτοῦ.

5 καὶ οὐκ ἐδύνατο ἐκεῖ ποιῆσαι οὐδεμίαν δύναμιν, εἰ μὴ ὀλίγοις ἀρρώστοις ἐπιθεὶς τὰς χεῖρας ἐθεράπευσεν·
6 καὶ ἐθαύμαζεν διὰ τὴν ἀπιστίαν αὐτῶν. Καὶ περιῆγεν τὰς κώμας κύκλῳ διδάσκων.

7 καὶ προσκαλεῖται τοὺς δώδεκα, καὶ ἤρξατο αὐτοὺς ἀποστέλλειν δύο δύο, καὶ ἐδίδου αὐτοῖς ἐξουσίαν τῶν πνευμάτων τῶν ἀκαθάρτων,
8 καὶ παρήγγειλεν αὐτοῖς ἵνα μηδὲν αἴρωσιν εἰς ὁδὸν εἰ μὴ ῥάβδον μόνον, μὴ ἄρτον, μὴ πήραν, μὴ εἰς τὴν ζώνην χαλκόν,
9 ἀλλὰ ὑποδεδεμένους σανδάλια,
καὶ μὴ ἐνδύσησθε δύο χιτῶνας.
10 καὶ ἔλεγεν αὐτοῖς·
Ὅπου ἐὰν εἰσέλθητε εἰς οἰκίαν, ἐκεῖ μένετε ἕως ἂν ἐξέλθητε ἐκεῖθεν.
11 καὶ ὃς ἂν τόπος μὴ δέξηται ὑμᾶς μηδὲ ἀκούσωσιν ὑμῶν, ἐκπορευόμενοι ἐκεῖθεν ἐκτινάξατε τὸν χοῦν τὸν ὑποκάτω τῶν ποδῶν ὑμῶν εἰς μαρτύριον αὐτοῖς.
12 Καὶ ἐξελθόντες ἐκήρυξαν ἵνα μετανοῶσιν,
13 καὶ δαιμόνια πολλὰ ἐξέβαλλον, καὶ ἤλειφον ἐλαίῳ πολλοὺς ἀρρώστους καὶ ἐθεράπευον.

[3] Is this not the craftsman, the son of Mary and brother of Jacob and Joses and Judas and Simon? *Yes!* And are not his sisters right here with us?" *Yes!* And they were taking offense at him. [4] And Jesus was saying to them this: "A prophet is not without honor except in his hometown and among his relatives and in his own house." [5] And he was not able to do there even one miracle, except after laying hands on a few sick ones, he healed them. [6] And he was marveling because of their lack of faith. And he we was going around the villages in a circuit teaching. [7] And he calls to the twelve, and he began to send them two-by-two, and he was giving them authority over unclean-spirits, [8] and he gave instructions to them that they should bring nothing on the road except a single staff, neither bread, nor purse, nor coin in the money belt, [9] but wearing the sandals, and "You *all* shall not wear two coats!" [10] And he was saying to them, "Wherever you enter into a house, there remain until you leave from there. [11] "And whichever place neither receives nor hears you, while departing from there, shake off the dust underneath your feet as testimony against them." [12] And after going out, they preached in order that they would repent. [13] And they were casting out many demons, and they were anointing with oil many sick people, and they were healing them.

14 Καὶ ἤκουσεν ὁ βασιλεὺς Ἡρῴδης, φανερὸν γὰρ ἐγένετο τὸ ὄνομα αὐτοῦ, καὶ ἔλεγον ὅτι
Ἰωάννης ὁ βαπτίζων ἐγήγερται ἐκ νεκρῶν, καὶ διὰ τοῦτο ἐνεργοῦσιν αἱ δυνάμεις ἐν αὐτῷ·
Ἠλίας ἐστίν·
ἄλλοι δὲ ἔλεγον ὅτι
προφήτης ὡς εἷς τῶν προφητῶν.

16 ἀκούσας δὲ ὁ Ἡρῴδης ἔλεγεν·
Ὃν ἐγὼ ἀπεκεφάλισα Ἰωάννην, οὗτος ἠγέρθη.

17 Αὐτὸς γὰρ ὁ Ἡρῴδης ἀποστείλας ἐκράτησεν τὸν Ἰωάννην καὶ ἔδησεν αὐτὸν ἐν φυλακῇ διὰ Ἡρῳδιάδα τὴν γυναῖκα Φιλίππου τοῦ ἀδελφοῦ αὐτοῦ, ὅτι αὐτὴν ἐγάμησεν·
18 ἔλεγεν γὰρ ὁ Ἰωάννης τῷ Ἡρῴδῃ ὅτι

Οὐκ ἔξεστίν σοι ἔχειν τὴν γυναῖκα τοῦ ἀδελφοῦ σου.

19 ἡ δὲ Ἡρῳδιὰς ἐνεῖχεν αὐτῷ καὶ ἤθελεν αὐτὸν ἀποκτεῖναι, καὶ οὐκ ἠδύνατο·
20 ὁ γὰρ Ἡρῴδης ἐφοβεῖτο τὸν Ἰωάννην, εἰδὼς αὐτὸν ἄνδρα δίκαιον καὶ ἅγιον, καὶ συνετήρει αὐτόν, καὶ ἀκούσας αὐτοῦ πολλὰ ἠπόρει, καὶ ἡδέως αὐτοῦ ἤκουεν.
21 Καὶ γενομένης ἡμέρας εὐκαίρου ὅτε Ἡρῴδης τοῖς γενεσίοις αὐτοῦ δεῖπνον ἐποίησεν τοῖς μεγιστᾶσιν αὐτοῦ καὶ τοῖς χιλιάρχοις καὶ τοῖς πρώτοις τῆς Γαλιλαίας,
22 καὶ εἰσελθούσης τῆς θυγατρὸς αὐτῆς τῆς Ἡρῳδιάδος καὶ ὀρχησαμένης καὶ ἀρεσάσης τῷ Ἡρῴδῃ καὶ τοῖς συνανακειμένοις, εἶπεν ὁ βασιλεὺς τῷ κορασίῳ·

Αἴτησόν με ὃ ἐὰν θέλῃς, καὶ δώσω σοι·
23 καὶ ὤμοσεν αὐτῇ·
Ὅ τι ἐάν με αἰτήσῃς δώσω σοι ἕως ἡμίσους τῆς βασιλείας μου.

14 And King Herod heard, for his name became known, and they were saying this: "John the one baptizing has been raised from the dead, and on account of this miracles
are working in him." 15 But others were saying this: "He is Elijah." Additionally, others were saying this: "He is a prophet, like one of the prophets."' 16 But after hearing,
Herod was saying, "John, whom I myself beheaded, this one is raised up." 17 For Herod himself, after sending after, seized John and bound him in prison for the sake of
Herodias, his brother Philip's wife, because he married her. 18 For John was saying to Herod this: "It is not allowed for you to have the wife of your brother." 19 Moreover,
Herodias was holding a grudge against him and was wanting to kill him, and she was not able; 20 for Herod was fearing John, knowing him *to be* a righteous and holy man,
and he was protecting him, and after hearing him about many things, he was growing perplexed and with pleasure he was listening to him. 21 And after an opportune day
happened, when Herod on his birthday made a dinner for his great men and for the military commanders and for the first men of Galilee, 22 and after the daughter of
Herodias entered and danced and pleased Herod and those reclining together, the king said to the young girl, "Ask me whatever you want, and I will give it to you." 23 And
he swore to her, "Whatever thing you ask me, I will give you up to half of my kingdom."

24 καὶ ἐξελθοῦσα εἶπεν τῇ μητρὶ αὐτῆς·
Τί αἰτήσωμαι;

ἡ δὲ εἶπεν·
Τὴν κεφαλὴν Ἰωάν-νου τοῦ βαπτίζοντος.

25 καὶ εἰσελθοῦσα εὐθὺς μετὰ σπουδῆς πρὸς τὸν βασιλέα ᾐτήσατο λέγουσα·
Θέλω ἵνα ἐξαυτῆς δῷς μοι ἐπὶ πίνακι τὴν κεφαλὴν Ἰωάννου τοῦ βαπτιστοῦ.

26 καὶ περίλυπος γενόμενος ὁ βασιλεὺς διὰ τοὺς ὅρκους καὶ τοὺς ἀνακειμένους οὐκ ἠθέλησεν ἀθετῆσαι αὐτήν·

27 καὶ εὐθὺς ἀποστείλας ὁ βασιλεὺς σπεκουλάτορα ἐπέταξεν ἐνέγκαι τὴν κεφαλὴν αὐτοῦ. καὶ ἀπελθὼν ἀπεκεφάλισεν αὐτὸν ἐν τῇ φυλακῇ
28 καὶ ἤνεγκεν τὴν κεφαλὴν αὐτοῦ ἐπὶ πίνακι καὶ ἔδωκεν αὐτὴν τῷ κορασίῳ, καὶ τὸ κοράσιον ἔδωκεν αὐτὴν τῇ μητρὶ αὐτῆς.

29 καὶ ἀκούσαντες οἱ μαθηταὶ αὐτοῦ ἦλθον καὶ ἦραν τὸ πτῶμα αὐτοῦ καὶ ἔθηκαν αὐτὸ ἐν μνημείῳ.

30 Καὶ συνάγονται οἱ ἀπόστολοι πρὸς τὸν Ἰησοῦν, καὶ ἀπήγγειλαν αὐτῷ πάντα ὅσα ἐποίησαν καὶ ὅσα ἐδίδαξαν.
31 καὶ λέγει αὐτοῖς·
Δεῦτε ὑμεῖς αὐτοὶ κατ᾽ ἰδίαν εἰς ἔρημον τόπον καὶ ἀναπαύσασθε ὀλίγον.
ἦσαν γὰρ οἱ ἐρχόμενοι καὶ οἱ ὑπάγοντες πολλοί, καὶ οὐδὲ φαγεῖν εὐκαίρουν.
32 καὶ ἀπῆλθον ἐν τῷ πλοίῳ εἰς ἔρημον τόπον κατ᾽ ἰδίαν.
33 καὶ εἶδον αὐτοὺς ὑπάγοντας καὶ ἐπέγνωσαν πολλοί, καὶ πεζῇ ἀπὸ πασῶν τῶν πόλεων συνέδραμον ἐκεῖ καὶ προῆλθον αὐτούς.

24 And after going out, she said to her mother, "What shall I ask for myself?" And she said, "The head of John, the one baptizing." 25 And after entering immediately with
haste to the king, she asked saying, "I want that right now you give me upon a platter the head of John the Baptist." 26 And after becoming deeply grieved, the king did not
want to refuse her on account of the vows and those reclining at dinner. 27 And immediately after sending after him, the king ordered an executioner to bring his head. And
after departing, he beheaded him in the prison 28 and he brought his head on a platter and gave it to the child, and the child gave it to her mother. 29 And after hearing, his
disciples came and took up his corpse and laid it in a tomb. 30 And the apostles gather together to Jesus, and they reported to him everything, how much they did, and how
much they taught. 31 And he says to them, "You yourselves come in private into a desolate place and rest a little." For the people coming and the people going away were
many, and moreover they were not having an opportunity to eat. 32 And they departed in the boat into a desolate place in private. 33 And they saw them departing and many
recognized *them*, and by land from all the cities, they ran together there and went in front of them.

34 καὶ ἐξελθὼν εἶδεν πο-
λὺν ὄχλον, καὶ ἐσπλαγ-
χνίσθη ἐπ' αὐτοὺς ὅτι
ἦσαν ὡς πρόβατα μὴ ἔχ-
οντα ποιμένα, καὶ ἤρξατο
διδάσκειν αὐτοὺς πολλά.
35 Καὶ ἤδη ὥρας πολλῆς
γενομένης προσελθόντες
αὐτῷ οἱ μαθηταὶ αὐτοῦ
ἔλεγον ὅτι

Ἔρημός ἐστιν ὁ
τόπος, καὶ ἤδη ὥρα
πολλή·
36 ἀπόλυσον αὐτούς, ἵνα
ἀπελθόντες εἰς τοὺς
κύκλῳ ἀγροὺς καὶ κώ-
μας ἀγοράσωσιν ἑαυ-
τοῖς τί φάγωσιν.

37 ὁ δὲ ἀποκριθεὶς
εἶπεν αὐτοῖς·

Δότε αὐτοῖς
ὑμεῖς φαγεῖν.

καὶ λέγουσιν αὐτῷ·

Ἀπελθόντες ἀγοράσωμεν δηναρίων διακο-
σίων ἄρτους καὶ δώσομεν αὐτοῖς φαγεῖν;

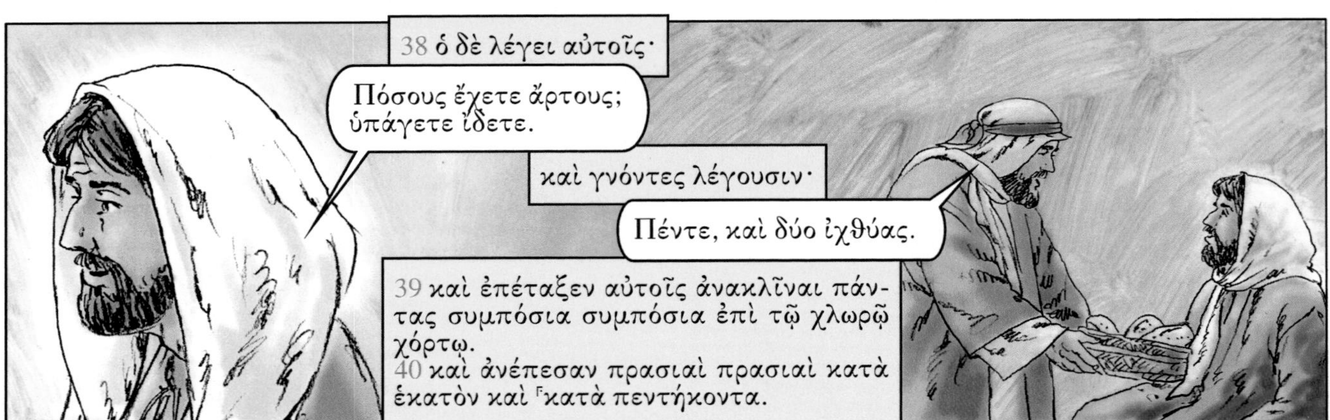
38 ὁ δὲ λέγει αὐτοῖς·
Πόσους ἔχετε ἄρτους; ὑπάγετε ἴδετε.
καὶ γνόντες λέγουσιν·
Πέντε, καὶ δύο ἰχθύας.
39 καὶ ἐπέταξεν αὐτοῖς ἀνακλῖναι πάντας συμπόσια συμπόσια ἐπὶ τῷ χλωρῷ
χόρτῳ.
40 καὶ ἀνέπεσαν πρασιαὶ πρασιαὶ κατὰ
ἑκατὸν καὶ ⸀κατὰ πεντήκοντα.

34 And after going out, he saw a great crowd, and he had compassion on them because they were like sheep not having a shepherd, and he began to teach them many things.
35 And when many hours had already passed by, after coming to him, the disciples were saying indeed, "The place is desolate, and already the hour *is* late; 36 send them
away, in order that, after departing into the surrounding fields and villages, they would buy for themselves something they should eat." 37 But he, answering back, said to
them, "You yourselves give them *something* to eat." And they say to him, "After departing, should we buy two hundred denarii worth of bread and we will give them *that*
to eat?" 38 But he says to them, "How many loaves do you have? Go look!" And after learning, they say, "Five, and two fish." 39 And he commanded them to all sit down
group by group upon the green grass. 40 And they sat down in companies, companies of a hundred and of fifty.

41 καὶ λαβὼν τοὺς πέντε ἄρτους
καὶ τοὺς δύο ἰχθύας ἀναβλέψας εἰς
τὸν οὐρανὸν εὐλόγησεν καὶ κατέ-
κλασεν τοὺς ἄρτους καὶ ἐδίδου
τοῖς μαθηταῖς αὐτοῦ ἵνα παρατιθῶσιν αὐτοῖς, καὶ τοὺς δύο
ἰχθύας ἐμέρισεν πᾶσιν.

42 καὶ ἔφαγον πάντες καὶ ἐχορτάσθησαν·
43 καὶ ἦραν κλάσματα δώδεκα κοφίνων πληρώματα καὶ ἀπὸ τῶν ἰχθύων.
44 καὶ ἦσαν οἱ φαγόντες τοὺς ἄρτους πεντακισχίλιοι ἄνδρες.

41 And after taking the five loaves and the two fish, looking up to heaven, he blessed and broke the loaves and he was giving to the disciples in order that they would set
the food before them, and the two fish he divided for all. 42 And they all ate and were filled. 43 And they took up broken pieces, twelve full baskets and from the fish.
44 And the ones eating the loaves were five thousand men.

45 Καὶ εὐθὺς ἠνάγκασεν τοὺς μαθητὰς αὐτοῦ ἐμ-βῆναι εἰς τὸ πλοῖον καὶ προάγειν εἰς τὸ πέραν πρὸς Βηθσαϊδάν, ἕως αὐ-τὸς ἀπολύει τὸν ὄχλον.

46 καὶ ἀποτα ά-μενος αὐτοῖς ἀπ-ῆλθεν εἰς τὸ ὄρος προσεύξασθαι.

47 Καὶ ὀψίας γενομένης ἦν τὸ πλοῖον ἐν μέσῳ τῆς θαλάσσης, καὶ αὐ-τὸς μόνος ἐπὶ τῆς γῆς.
48 καὶ ἰδὼν αὐτοὺς βα-σανιζομένους ἐν τῷ ἐλ-αύνειν, ἦν γὰρ ὁ ἄν-εμος ἐναντίος αὐτοῖς, περὶ τετάρτην φυλακὴν τῆς νυκτὸς ἔρχεται πρὸς αὐ-τοὺς περιπατῶν ἐπὶ τῆς θαλάσσης· καὶ ἤθελεν παρελθεῖν αὐτούς.

49 οἱ δὲ ἰδόντες αὐτὸν ἐπὶ τῆς θαλάσσης πε-ριπατοῦντα ἔδοξαν ὅτι φάντασμά ἐστιν καὶ ἀνέκραξαν,
50 πάντες γὰρ αὐτὸν εἶδον καὶ ἐταράχθη-σαν. ὁ δὲ εὐθὺς ἐλά-λησεν μετ᾽ αὐτῶν, καὶ λέγει αὐτοῖς·
Θαρσεῖτε, ἐγώ εἰμι, μὴ φοβεῖσθε.

51 καὶ ἀνέβη πρὸς αὐτοὺς εἰς τὸ πλοῖον, καὶ ἐκόπασεν ὁ ἄνεμος. καὶ λίαν ἐκ περισσοῦ ἐν ἑαυτοῖς ἐξίσταντο,
52 οὐ γὰρ συνῆκαν ἐπὶ τοῖς ἄρτοις, ἀλλ᾽ ἦν αὐτῶν ἡ καρδία πεπωρωμένη.

53 Καὶ διαπεράσαντες ἐπὶ τὴν γῆν ἦλθον εἰς Γεννησα-ρὲτ καὶ προσωρμίσθησαν.
54 καὶ ἐξελθόντων αὐτῶν ἐκ τοῦ πλοίου εὐθὺς ἐπιγνόν-τες αὐτὸν
55 περιέδραμον ὅλην τὴν χώραν ἐκείνην καὶ ἤρξαντο ἐπὶ τοῖς κραβάττοις τοὺς κακῶς ἔχοντας περιφέρειν ὅπου ἤκουον ὅτι ἐστίν.

45 And straightaway he compelled his disciples to embark in the boat and to go ahead to the other side to Bethsaida, until he himself released the crowd. 46 And after
leaving them, he departed into the mountain to pray. 47 And when evening came, the boat was in the middle of the sea, and he was alone on the land. 48 And after seeing
them struggling while rowing, for the wind was opposed to them, around the fourth watch of the night he comes toward them walking upon the sea; and he wanted to come
alongside them. 49 Well, they, after seeing him walking on the sea, thought that it was an apparition and they cried out, 50 for they all saw him and were troubled. Well, he
straightaway spoke with them, and he says to them, "Be courageous! I am he. Do not be afraid!" 51 And he went up to them into the boat, and the wind ceased. And very
much they were astounded among themselves; 52 for they had not understood about the loaves, but the heart of theirs was hardened. 53 And after crossing over upon the
land, they went into Gennesaret and anchored on the land. 54 And after they went out of the boat, straightaway after recognizing him 55 they ran around that whole region
and began to carry about on the beds the ones having it badly to where they were hearing that he was.

56 καὶ ὅπου ἂν εἰσεπορεύετο εἰς κώμας ἢ εἰς πόλεις ἢ εἰς ἀγροὺς ἐν ταῖς ἀγοραῖς ἐτίθεσαν τοὺς ἀσθενοῦντας, καὶ παρεκάλουν αὐτὸν ἵνα κἂν τοῦ κρασπέδου τοῦ ἱματίου αὐτοῦ ἅψωνται· καὶ ὅσοι ἂν ἥψαντο αὐτοῦ ἐσῴζοντο.

Κεφ.
Ζ´

1 Καὶ συνάγονται πρὸς αὐτὸν οἱ Φαρισαῖοι καί τινες τῶν γραμματέων ἐλθόντες ἀπὸ Ἱεροσολύμων
2 καὶ ἰδόντες τινὰς τῶν μαθητῶν αὐτοῦ ὅτι κοιναῖς χερσίν, τοῦτ᾽ ἔστιν ἀνίπτοις, ἐσθίουσιν τοὺς ἄρτους—
3 οἱ γὰρ Φαρισαῖοι καὶ πάντες οἱ Ἰουδαῖοι ἐὰν μὴ πυγμῇ νίψωνται τὰς χεῖρας οὐκ ἐσθίουσιν, κρατοῦντες τὴν παράδοσιν τῶν πρεσβυτέρων,
4 καὶ ἀπ᾽ ἀγορᾶς ἐὰν μὴ βαπτίσωνται οὐκ ἐσθίουσιν, καὶ ἄλλα πολλά ἐστιν ἃ παρέλαβον κρατεῖν, βαπτισμοὺς ποτηρίων καὶ ξεστῶν καὶ χαλκίων καὶ κλινῶν—
5 καὶ ἐπερωτῶσιν αὐτὸν οἱ Φαρισαῖοι καὶ οἱ γραμματεῖς·

Διὰ τί οὐ περιπατοῦσιν οἱ μαθηταί σου κατὰ τὴν παράδοσιν τῶν πρεσβυτέρων, ἀλλὰ κοιναῖς χερσὶν ἐσθίουσιν τὸν ἄρτον;

6 ὁ δὲ εἶπεν αὐτοῖς·

Καλῶς ἐπροφήτευσεν Ἠσαΐας περὶ ὑμῶν τῶν ὑποκριτῶν, ὡς γέγραπται ὅτι

Οὗτος ὁ λαὸς τοῖς χείλεσίν με τιμᾷ, ἡ δὲ καρδία αὐτῶν πόρρω ἀπέχει ἀπ᾽ ἐμοῦ·
7 μάτην δὲ σέβονταί με, διδάσκοντες διδασκαλίας ἐντάλματα ἀνθρώπων·

8 ἀφέντες τὴν ἐντολὴν τοῦ θεοῦ κρατεῖτε τὴν παράδοσιν τῶν ἀνθρώπων.

[56] And wherever he entered into villages or into cities or into the fields, they were setting the sick in the marketplaces, and were imploring him in order that they would touch even just the border of his outer garment; and however many touched him were being restored. 7:1 And the Pharisees gather to him and some of the scribes coming from Jerusalem [2] and, after noticing some of his disciples that with defiled hands (that is, unwashed) they were eating the loaves of bread - [3] for the Pharisees and all the Judeans, unless from elbow to knuckles they wash their hands, they do not eat, holding the tradition of the elders; [4] also from the marketplace, unless they wash themselves, they do not eat; and there are many other things that they received to hold onto: washings of cups and jars and brass vessels and seats - [5] and the Pharisees and the scribes are asking him, "For what reason are your disciples not living according to the tradition of the elders, but with defiled hands they are eating the bread?" [6] So, he said to them, "Isaiah prophesied well about you hypocrites, as it has been written *like* this: 'This people honors me with their lips, but their heart is far removed from me. [7] Moreover, in vain they worship me, teaching teachings, doctrines of people'; [8] after leaving the command of God, you are holding onto the tradition of people."

α εγεν α το ς·

Καλῶς ἀθετεῖτε τὴν ἐντο-
λὴν τοῦ θεοῦ, ἵνα τὴν παράδοσιν
ὑμῶν τηρήσητε·
10 Μωϋσῆς γὰρ εἶπεν· Τίμα τὸν
πατέρα σου καὶ τὴν μητέρα σου,
καί· Ὁ κακολογῶν πατέρα ἢ μητέρα θανάτῳ τελευτάτω·
11 ὑμεῖς δὲ λέγετε· Ἐὰν εἴπῃ
ἄνθρωπος τῷ πατρὶ ἢ τῇ μητρί·
Κορβᾶν, ὅ ἐστιν Δῶρον, ὃ ἐὰν ἐξ
ἐμοῦ ὠφεληθῇς,
12 οὐκέτι ἀφίετε αὐτὸν οὐδὲν
ποιῆσαι τῷ πατρὶ ἢ τῇ μητρί,
13 ἀκυροῦντες τὸν λόγον τοῦ
θεοῦ τῇ παραδόσει ὑμῶν ᾗ παρε-
δώκατε· καὶ παρόμοια τοιαῦτα
πολλὰ ποιεῖτε.

14 Καὶ προσκαλεσάμενος πάλιν
τὸν ὄχλον ἔλεγεν αὐτοῖς·
Ἀκούσατέ μου πάντες καὶ σύνετε.
15 οὐδέν ἐστιν ἔξωθεν τοῦ ἀνθρώπου
εἰσπορευόμενον εἰς αὐτὸν ὃ δύναται
κοινῶσαι αὐτόν· ἀλλὰ τὰ ἐκ τοῦ ἀνθρώπου
ἐκπορευόμενά ἐστιν τὰ κοινοῦντα τὸν ἄνθρωπον.
16 [Εἴ τις ἔχει ὦτα ἀκούειν ἀκουέτω.]

17 Καὶ ὅτε εἰσῆλθεν εἰς
οἶκον ἀπὸ τοῦ ὄχλου, ἐπηρώτων αὐτὸν οἱ μαθηταὶ αὐτοῦ
τὴν παραβολήν.
18 καὶ λέγει αὐτοῖς·
Οὕτως καὶ ὑμεῖς ἀσύ-
νετοί ἐστε; οὐ νοεῖτε ὅτι πᾶν
τὸ ἔξωθεν εἰσπορευόμενον
εἰς τὸν ἄνθρωπον οὐ δύναται
αὐτὸν κοινῶσαι,

9 And he was saying to them, "You are rejecting well the commandment of God, in order that you would keep your tradition. 10 For Moses said, 'Honor your father and
your mother' and 'The one speaking evil of father or mother, let him end in death.' 11 But you yourselves are saying, 'If a person says to his father or his mother, '*It is*
Corban (which is a gift), whatever you are owed from me,' 12 then you are no longer letting him to do even one thing for his father or his mother, 13 *thereby* invalidating
the word of God by your tradition, which you have handed on, and you are *regularly* doing many such similar things as these." 14 And, after calling the crowd again, he
was saying to them, "All of you listen to me and understand! 15 There is not one thing from outside of a person entering into him that is able to defile him; but the things
coming out of the person are the things defiling the person. 16 If someone has ears to be listening, let him keep listening." 17 And when he entered into a house away from
the crowd, his disciples were asking him about the parable. 18 And he proceeds saying to them, "In this way, are also you yourselves without understanding? Don't you
understand that everything outside entering into the person is not able defile him,

19 ὅτι οὐκ εἰσπορεύεται
αὐτοῦ εἰς τὴν καρδίαν ἀλλ᾽ εἰς
τὴν κοιλίαν, καὶ εἰς τὸν ἀφεδ-
ρῶνα ἐκπορεύεται;

—καθαρίζων πάντα τὰ βρώ-
ματα.
20 ἔλεγεν δὲ ὅτι

Τὸ ἐκ τοῦ ἀνθρώπου ἐκπορευό-
μενον ἐκεῖνο κοινοῖ τὸν ἄνθρω-
πον·
21 ἔσωθεν γὰρ ἐκ τῆς καρδίας
τῶν ἀνθρώπων οἱ διαλογισμοὶ οἱ
κακοὶ ἐκπορεύονται, πορνεῖαι,
κλοπαί, φόνοι,
22 μοιχεῖαι, πλεονεξίαι, πονη-
ρίαι, δόλος, ἀσέλγεια, ὀφθαλμὸς
πονηρός, βλασφημία, ὑπερηφα-
νία, ἀφροσύνη·
23 πάντα ταῦτα τὰ πονηρὰ ἔσωθεν ἐκπορεύεται καὶ κοινοῖ τὸν
ἄνθρωπον.

24 Ἐκεῖθεν δὲ ἀναστὰς
ἀπῆλθεν εἰς τὰ ὅρια Τύ-
ρου. καὶ εἰσελθὼν εἰς
οἰκίαν οὐδένα ἤθελεν
γνῶναι, καὶ οὐκ ἠδυνή-
θη λαθεῖν·
25 ἀλλ᾽ εὐθὺς ἀκούσασα
γυνὴ περὶ αὐτοῦ, ἧς εἶχ-
εν τὸ θυγάτριον αὐτῆς
πνεῦμα ἀκάθαρτον, ἐλ-
θοῦσα προσέπεσεν πρὸς
τοὺς πόδας αὐτοῦ·

26 ἡ δὲ γυνὴ ἦν Ἑλληνίς, Συ-
ροφοινίκισσα τῷ γένει· καὶ
ἠρώτα αὐτὸν ἵνα τὸ δαιμό-
νιον ἐκβάλῃ ἐκ τῆς θυγατ-
ρὸς αὐτῆς.
27 καὶ ἔλεγεν αὐτῇ·

Ἄφες πρῶτον χορτασ-
θῆναι τὰ τέκνα, οὐ γὰρ
καλόν ἐστιν λαβεῖν τὸν ἄρτον τῶν τέκνων καὶ τοῖς κυ-
ναρίοις βαλεῖν.

28 ἡ δὲ ἀπεκρίθη καὶ λέγει αὐτῷ·

Κύριε, καὶ τὰ κυ-
νάρια ὑποκάτω τῆς τρα-
πέζης ἐσθίουσιν ἀπὸ
τῶν ψιχίων τῶν παιδίων.

19 because it does not enter into his heart but into his belly, and it goes out into the toilet?" *Surely, yes!* - (*He was* making all foods clean.) 20 Additionally, he was saying
this: "The thing coming out of the person, that defiles the person. 21 For from within out of the heart of people, evil thoughts come out, fornications, thefts, murders,
22 adulteries, greeds, evils, deceit, debaucheries, an evil eye, blasphemy, pride, foolishness: 23 all these evil things from within come out and defile the person." 24 Well,
from there, after standing up, he departed into the region of Tyre. And after entering into a house, he was not wanting anyone to know, and he was not able to escape
notice. 25 But straightaway a woman, after hearing about him, whose little daughter of hers was having an unclean spirit, coming, fell down at his feet. 26 Moreover, the
woman was a Greek, Syrophoenician in race; and she was asking him that he would cast out the demon from her daughter. 27 And he was saying to her, "Let the children
first be satisfied, for it is not good to take the children's bread and to throw it to the dogs." 28 Well, she answered back and says to him, "Lord, even the dogs under the
table eat from the crumbs of the little children."

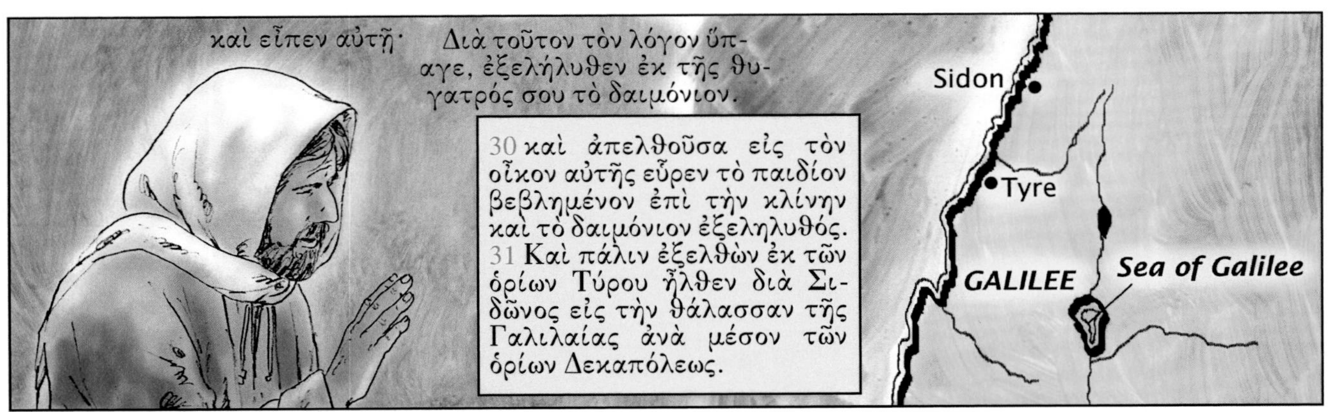
καὶ εἶπεν αὐτῇ·
Διὰ τοῦτον τὸν λόγον ὕπ-
αγε, ἐξελήλυθεν ἐκ τῆς θυ-
γατρός σου τὸ δαιμόνιον.
30 καὶ ἀπελθοῦσα εἰς τὸν
οἶκον αὐτῆς εὗρεν τὸ παιδίον
βεβλημένον ἐπὶ τὴν κλίνην
καὶ τὸ δαιμόνιον ἐξεληλυθός.
31 Καὶ πάλιν ἐξελθὼν ἐκ τῶν
ὁρίων Τύρου ἦλθεν διὰ Σι-
δῶνος εἰς τὴν θάλασσαν τῆς
Γαλιλαίας ἀνὰ μέσον τῶν
ὁρίων Δεκαπόλεως.
Sidon
Tyre
GALILEE
Sea of Galilee

32 καὶ φέρουσιν αὐτῷ
κωφὸν καὶ μογιλάλον,
καὶ παρακαλοῦσιν αὐ-
τὸν ἵνα ἐπιθῇ αὐτῷ
τὴν χεῖρα.
33 καὶ ἀπολαβόμενος
αὐτὸν ἀπὸ τοῦ ὄχλου
κατ' ἰδίαν

ἔβαλεν τοὺς δακτύλους αὐτοῦ
εἰς τὰ ὦτα αὐτοῦ καὶ πτύσας
ἥψατο τῆς γλώσσης αὐτοῦ,

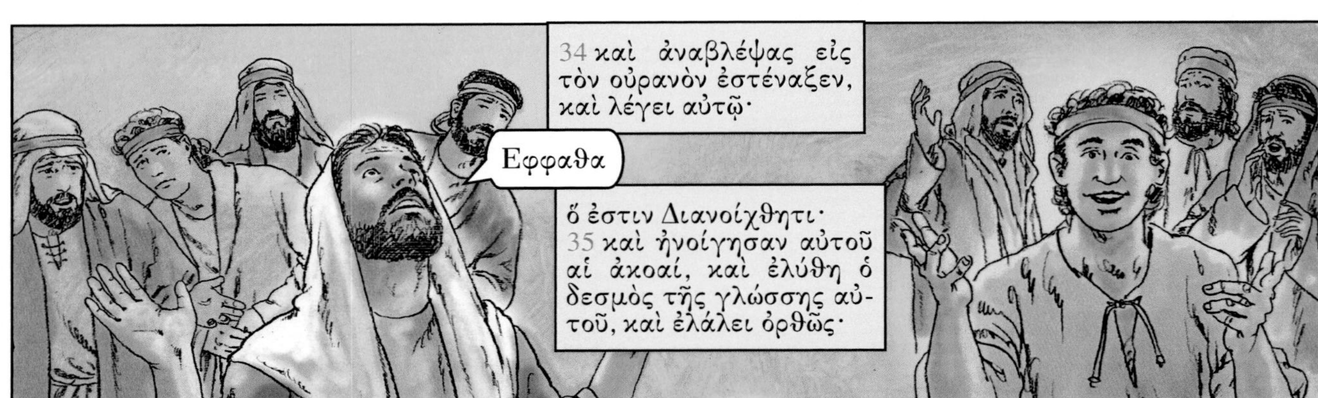
34 καὶ ἀναβλέψας εἰς
τὸν οὐρανὸν ἐστέναξεν,
καὶ λέγει αὐτῷ·
Εφφαθα
ὅ ἐστιν Διανοίχθητι·
35 καὶ ἠνοίγησαν αὐτοῦ
αἱ ἀκοαί, καὶ ἐλύθη ὁ
δεσμὸς τῆς γλώσσης αὐ-
τοῦ, καὶ ἐλάλει ὀρθῶς·

36 καὶ διεστείλατο αὐτοῖς
ἵνα μηδενὶ λέγωσιν· ὅσον
δὲ αὐτοῖς διεστέλλετο,
αὐτοὶ μᾶλλον περισσότε-
ρον ἐκήρυσσον.
37 καὶ ὑπερπερισσῶς ἐξ-
επλήσσοντο λέγοντες·
Καλῶς πάντα πεποί-
ηκεν, καὶ τοὺς κωφοὺς
ποιεῖ ἀκούειν καὶ ἀλάλους
λαλεῖν.

[29] And he said to her, "Because of this very word, go, the demon has come out from your daughter." [30] And after departing into her house, she found her little child having been laid upon the bed and the demon having come out. [31] And again after going out from the region of Tyre, he went through Sidon to the sea of Galilee, through the middle of the region of Decapolis. [32] And they bring to him a deaf and mute man, and they strongly urge him that he would lay a hand on him. [33] And after taking him aside from the crowd in private, he put his fingers into his ears, and, after spitting, he touched his tongue, [34] and, after looking up to heaven, he sighed, and he says to him, "Ephphatha," that is, "Be opened." [35] And his ears were opened, and the binding of his tongue was loosened, and he proceeds speaking correctly. [36] And he commanded them that they would speak to no one; but as much as he was commanding them, they themselves more profusely were proclaiming it. [37] And beyond measure they were being astonished saying, "He has done all things well; both the deaf he makes to hear and the mute to speak."

Κεφ.
Θ´

1 Ἐν ἐκείναις ταῖς ἡμέραις πάλιν πολλοῦ ὄχλου ὄντος καὶ μὴ ἐχόντων τί φάγωσιν, προσκαλεσάμενος τοὺς μαθητὰς λέγει αὐτοῖς·

2 Σπλαγχνίζομαι ἐπὶ τὸν ὄχλον ὅτι ἤδη ἡμέραι τρεῖς προσμένουσίν μοι καὶ οὐκ ἔχουσιν τί φάγωσιν·
3 καὶ ἐὰν ἀπολύσω αὐτοὺς νήστεις εἰς οἶκον αὐτῶν, ἐκλυθήσονται ἐν τῇ ὁδῷ· καί τινες αὐτῶν ἀπὸ μακρόθεν ἥκασιν.

4 καὶ ἀπεκρίθησαν αὐτῷ οἱ μαθηταὶ αὐτοῦ ὅτι
Πόθεν τούτους δυνήσεταί τις ὧδε χορτάσαι ἄρτων ἐπ' ἐρημίας;
5 καὶ ἠρώτα αὐτούς·
Πόσους ἔχετε ἄρτους;

οἱ δὲ εἶπαν·
Ἑπτά.

6 καὶ παραγγέλλει τῷ ὄχλῳ ἀναπεσεῖν ἐπὶ τῆς γῆς· καὶ λαβὼν τοὺς ἑπτὰ ἄρτους εὐχαριστήσας ἔκλασεν καὶ ἐδίδου τοῖς μαθηταῖς αὐτοῦ ἵνα παρατιθῶσιν καὶ παρέθηκαν τῷ ὄχλῳ.
7 καὶ εἶχον ἰχθύδια ὀλίγα· καὶ εὐλογήσας αὐτὰ εἶπεν καὶ ταῦτα παρατιθέναι.
8 καὶ ἔφαγον καὶ ἐχορτάσθησαν, καὶ ἦραν περισσεύματα κλασμάτων ἑπτὰ σπυρίδας.
9 ἦσαν δὲ ὡς τετρακισχίλιοι. καὶ ἀπέλυσεν αὐτούς.

8:1 In those days, again while there was a large crowd and they were not having what they should eat, after calling the disciples, he begins saying to them, 2 “I have compassion for the crowd, because already three days they are remaining with me and they are not having what they should eat; 3 and, if I release them hungry to their home,
they will faint on the way; and some of them have come from far away.” 4 And his disciples answered back to him this: “From where will someone here be able to feed
them loaves of bread in a desert?” 5 And he was asking them, “How many loaves do you have?” So they said, “Seven.” 6 And he commands the crowd to sit down upon
the ground; and, after taking the seven loaves, giving thanks, he broke them and was giving *them* to his disciples, in order that they would serve and they served the crowd.
7 And they were having a few fishes; and, after blessing them, he said also to serve them. 8 And they ate and were filled, and they picked up extra portions of the pieces,
seven baskets! 9 Moreover, there were about four thousand and he released them.

10 καὶ εὐθὺς ἐμβὰς εἰς τὸ πλοῖον μετὰ τῶν μαθητῶν αὐτοῦ ἦλθεν εἰς τὰ μέρη Δαλμανουθά.
11 Καὶ ἐξῆλθον οἱ Φαρισαῖοι καὶ ἤρξαντο συζητεῖν αὐτῷ, ζητοῦντες παρ' αὐτοῦ σημεῖον ἀπὸ τοῦ οὐρανοῦ, πειράζοντες αὐτόν.
12 καὶ ἀναστενάξας τῷ πνεύματι αὐτοῦ λέγει·
Τί ἡ γενεὰ αὕτη ζητεῖ σημεῖον; ἀμὴν λέγω ὑμῖν, εἰ δοθήσεται τῇ γενεᾷ ταύτῃ σημεῖον.

13 καὶ ἀφεὶς αὐτοὺς πάλιν ἐμβὰς ἀπῆλθεν εἰς τὸ πέραν.

14 Καὶ ἐπελάθοντο λαβεῖν ἄρτους, καὶ εἰ μὴ ἕνα ἄρτον οὐκ εἶχον μεθ' ἑαυτῶν ἐν τῷ πλοίῳ.
15 καὶ διεστέλλετο αὐτοῖς λέγων·
Ὁρᾶτε, βλέπετε ἀπὸ τῆς ζύμης τῶν Φαρισαίων καὶ τῆς ζύμης Ἡρῴδου.
16 καὶ διελογίζοντο πρὸς ἀλλήλους ὅτι ἄρτους οὐκ ἔχουσιν.
17 καὶ γνοὺς λέγει αὐτοῖς·
Τί διαλογίζεσθε ὅτι ἄρτους οὐκ ἔχετε; οὔπω νοεῖτε οὐδὲ συνίετε; πεπωρωμένην ἔχετε τὴν καρδίαν ὑμῶν;
18 ὀφθαλμοὺς ἔχοντες οὐ βλέπετε καὶ ὦτα ἔχοντες οὐκ ἀκούετε;

καὶ οὐ μνημονεύετε
19 ὅτε τοὺς πέντε ἄρτους ἔκλασα εἰς τοὺς πεντακισχιλίους, πόσους κοφίνους κλασμάτων πλήρεις ἤρατε;
λέγουσιν αὐτῷ·
Δώδεκα.
20 ὅτε καὶ τοὺς ἑπτὰ εἰς τοὺς τετρακισχιλίους, πόσων σπυρίδων πληρώματα κλασμάτων ἤρατε;
καὶ λέγουσιν αὐτῷ·
Ἑπτά.
21 καὶ ἔλεγεν αὐτοῖς·
Οὔπω συνίετε;

[10] And straightaway, after embarking into the boat with his disciples, he came into the parts of Dalmanutha. [11] And the Pharisees came out and they began to dispute with
him, seeking from him a sign from heaven, testing him. [12] And, after sighing deeply in his spirit, he says, “Why is this generation seeking a sign? Amen! I am saying to
you, if a sign will be given to this generation.” [13] And, after leaving them, embarking again, he departed to the other side. [14] And they forgot to take loaves, and except for
one loaf, they were not having anything with them in the boat. [15] And was commanding them saying, “Watch out, be aware of the leaven of the Pharisees and the leaven
of Herod.” [16] And they were arguing with one another, because they did not have the loaves. [17] And knowing he says to them, “Why are you arguing because you do not
loaves? Don’t you yet know nor understand? *Surely, yes!* Are you holding a hardened heart?! [18] *Although* having eyes, don’t you see, and having ears, don’t you hear?
Surely, yes! And don’t you remember [19] when I broke the five loaves for the five thousand, how many baskets full of broken pieces you gathered?” *Surely, yes!* They say
to him, “Twelve.” [20] “Also when the seven for the four thousand, the extras of how many basketfuls of broken pieces did you gather?” And they say to him, “Seven.”
[21] And he was saying to them, “Don’t you yet understand?” *Surely, yes!*

22 Καὶ ἔρχονται εἰς Βηθσαϊδάν. καὶ φέρουσιν αὐτῷ τυφλὸν καὶ παρακαλοῦσιν αὐτὸν ἵνα αὐτοῦ ἅψηται.
23 καὶ ἐπιλαβόμενος τῆς χειρὸς τοῦ τυφλοῦ ἐξήνεγκεν αὐτὸν ἔξω τῆς κώμης, καὶ πτύσας εἰς τὰ ὄμματα αὐτοῦ, ἐπιθεὶς τὰς χεῖρας αὐτῷ, ἐπηρώτα αὐτόν·

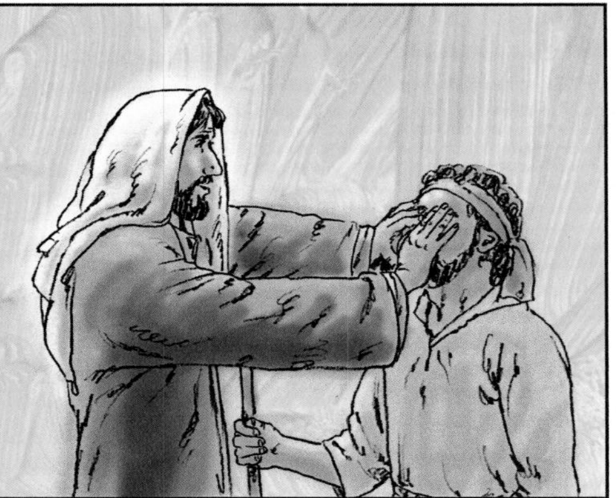

Εἴ τι βλέπεις;
24 καὶ ἀναβλέψας ἔλεγεν·
Βλέπω τοὺς ἀνθρώπους ὅτι ὡς δένδρα ὁρῶ περιπατοῦντας.

25 εἶτα πάλιν ἐπέθηκεν τὰς χεῖρας ἐπὶ τοὺς ὀφθαλμοὺς αὐτοῦ, καὶ διέβλεψεν καὶ ἀπεκατέστη καὶ ἐνέβλεπεν τηλαυγῶς ἅπαντα.

26 καὶ ἀπέστειλεν αὐτὸν εἰς οἶκον αὐτοῦ λέγων·
Μηδὲ εἰς τὴν κώμην εἰσέλθῃς.

27 Καὶ ἐξῆλθεν ὁ Ἰησοῦς καὶ οἱ μαθηταὶ αὐτοῦ εἰς τὰς κώμας Καισαρείας τῆς Φιλίππου· καὶ ἐν τῇ ὁδῷ ἐπηρώτα τοὺς μαθητὰς αὐτοῦ λέγων αὐτοῖς·
Τίνα με λέγουσιν οἱ ἄνθρωποι εἶναι;
28 οἱ δὲ εἶπαν αὐτῷ λέγοντες ὅτι
Ἰωάννην τὸν βαπτιστήν, καὶ ἄλλοι Ἠλίαν, ἄλλοι δὲ ὅτι εἷς τῶν προφητῶν.

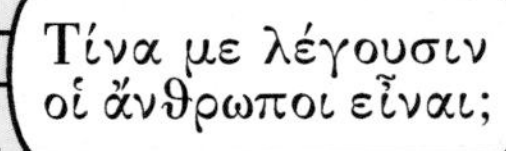

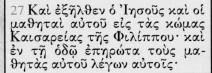

29 καὶ αὐτὸς ἐπηρώτα αὐτούς·
Ὑμεῖς δὲ τίνα με λέγετε εἶναι;
ἀποκριθεὶς ὁ Πέτρος λέγει αὐτῷ·
Σὺ εἶ ὁ χριστός.

30 καὶ ἐπετίμησεν αὐτοῖς ἵνα μηδενὶ λέγωσιν περὶ αὐτοῦ.

[22] And they come into Bethsaida. And they bring to him a blind man and they beg him in order that he would touch him. [23] And after taking the hand of the blind man, he brought him out outside of the village, and, after spitting into his eyes, laying his hands upon him, he was asking him, "Are you seeing something?" [24] And, after looking up, he was saying, "I see people that I observe walking around like trees." [25] Then again he laid his hands upon his eyes, and he looked intently and was restored and he was looking clearly at all things. [26] And he sent him away to his home saying, "Do not even enter into the village." [27] And Jesus went out, and his disciples, into the villages of Caesarea of Philip; and on the way he was asking his disciples, saying to them, "Whom do persons say that I am?" [28] Well, they told him saying this: "John the Baptist, and others, Elijah, moreover, others, that you are one of the prophets." [29] And he himself was asking them, "But you yourselves, whom do you say that I am?" Answering back, Peter says to him, "You yourself are the Messiah." [30] And he commanded them that they should speak about him to no one.

31 Καὶ ἤρξατο διδάσκειν
αὐτοὺς ὅτι δεῖ τὸν υἱὸν
τοῦ ἀνθρώπου πολλὰ πα-
θεῖν καὶ ἀποδοκιμασθῆ-
ναι ὑπὸ τῶν πρεσβυτέρων
καὶ τῶν ἀρχιερέων καὶ τῶν
γραμματέων καὶ ἀποκταν-
θῆναι καὶ μετὰ τρεῖς ἡμέ-
ρας ἀναστῆναι·
32 καὶ παρρησίᾳ τὸν λό-
γον ἐλάλει. καὶ προσλαβό-
μενος ὁ Πέτρος αὐτὸν
ἤρξατο ἐπιτιμᾶν αὐτῷ.

33 ὁ δὲ ἐπιστραφεὶς καὶ
ἰδὼν τοὺς μαθητὰς αὐτοῦ
ἐπετίμησεν Πέτρῳ καὶ
λέγει·

Ὕπαγε ὀπίσω μου, Σατα-
νᾶ, ὅτι οὐ φρονεῖς τὰ τοῦ θεοῦ
ἀλλὰ τὰ τῶν ἀνθρώπων.

34 Καὶ προσκαλεσάμενος τὸν
ὄχλον σὺν τοῖς μαθηταῖς αὐτοῦ
εἶπεν αὐτοῖς·

Εἴ τις θέλει ὀπίσω μου ἐλθεῖν,
ἀπαρνησάσθω ἑαυτὸν καὶ ἀράτω
τὸν σταυρὸν αὐτοῦ καὶ ἀκολου-
θείτω μοι.
35 ὃς γὰρ ἐὰν θέλῃ τὴν ψυχὴν
αὐτοῦ σῶσαι ἀπολέσει αὐτήν· ὃς
δ᾽ ἂν ἀπολέσει τὴν ψυχὴν αὐτοῦ
ἕνεκεν ἐμοῦ καὶ τοῦ εὐαγγελίου
σώσει αὐτήν.
36 τί γὰρ ὠφελεῖ ἄνθρωπον
κερδῆσαι τὸν κόσμον ὅλον καὶ
ζημιωθῆναι τὴν ψυχὴν αὐτοῦ;
37 τί γὰρ δοῖ ἄνθρωπος ἀντάλ-
λαγμα τῆς ψυχῆς αὐτοῦ;
38 ὃς γὰρ ἐὰν ἐπαισχυνθῇ με καὶ
τοὺς ἐμοὺς λόγους ἐν τῇ γενεᾷ
ταύτῃ τῇ μοιχαλίδι καὶ ἁμαρ-
τωλῷ, καὶ ὁ υἱὸς τοῦ ἀνθρώπου
ἐπαισχυνθήσεται αὐτὸν ὅταν
ἔλθῃ ἐν τῇ δόξῃ τοῦ πατρὸς
αὐτοῦ μετὰ τῶν ἀγγέλων τῶν
ἁγίων.

Κεφ. Ι´

1 καὶ ἔλεγεν αὐτοῖς·

Ἀμὴν λέγω ὑμῖν ὅτι εἰσίν τινες
τῶν ὧδε ἑστηκότων οἵτινες οὐ μὴ
γεύσωνται θανάτου ἕως ἂν ἴδωσιν τὴν βασιλείαν τοῦ θεοῦ
ἐληλυθυῖαν ἐν δυνάμει.

[31] And he began to teach them that the Son of Man must suffer many things and be rejected by the elders and the chief priests and the scribes and be killed and after three
days rise again. [32] And in a forthright way he was addressing the matter. And, after taking hold of him, Peter began rebuking him. [33] Then, he, after turning around and
seeing his disciples, rebuked Peter and says, “Get behind me, Satan, because you do not consider the things of God, but the things of people.” [34] And after calling the
crowd with his disciples, he said to them, “If anyone wants to go behind me, let him deny himself and let him take up his cross and let him be following me. [35] For whoever
wants to save his life will lose it; but whoever loses his life on account of me and of the gospel will save it. [36] For what profits a person to gain the whole world and to
forfeit his soul? [37] For what does a person give in exchange for his soul? [38] For whoever is ashamed of me and of my words in this adulterous and sinful generation, the
Son of Man also will be ashamed of him whenever he comes in the glory of his Father with the holy angels.” 9:1 And he was speaking to them, “Amen! I am saying to
you that there are some of the ones standing here, who will never ever taste death until they see the kingdom of God having come in power.”

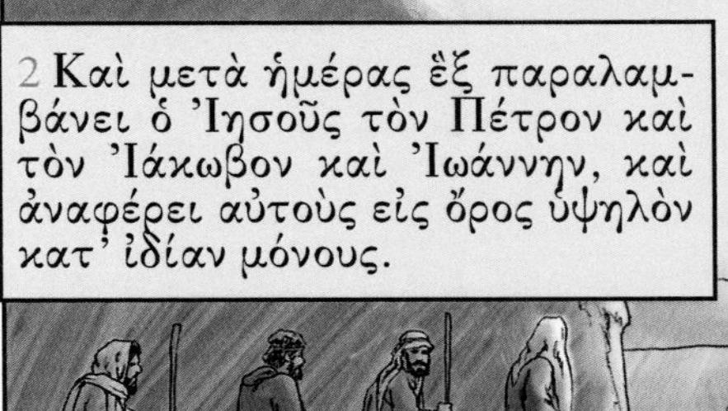
2 Καὶ μετὰ ἡμέρας ἓξ παραλαμ-
βάνει ὁ Ἰησοῦς τὸν Πέτρον καὶ
τὸν Ἰάκωβον καὶ Ἰωάννην, καὶ
ἀναφέρει αὐτοὺς εἰς ὄρος ὑψηλὸν
κατ᾽ ἰδίαν μόνους.

ἔμπροσθεν αὐ-
τῶν,
3 καὶ τὰ ἱμάτια
αὐτοῦ ἐγένετο
στίλβοντα λευ-
κὰ λίαν οἷα γνα-
φεὺς ἐπὶ τῆς γῆς
οὐ δύναται οὔ-
τως λευκᾶναι.
4 καὶ ὤφθη αὐ-
τοῖς Ἠλίας σὺν
Μωϋσεῖ, καὶ ἦ-
σαν συλλαλοῦν-
τες τῷ Ἰησοῦ.

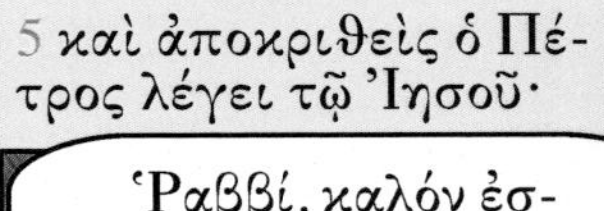
5 καὶ ἀποκριθεὶς ὁ Πέ-
τρος λέγει τῷ Ἰησοῦ·

Ῥαββί, καλόν ἐσ-
τιν ἡμᾶς ὧδε εἶναι, καὶ
ποιήσωμεν τρεῖς σκηνάς,
σοὶ μίαν καὶ Μωϋσεῖ
μίαν καὶ Ἠλίᾳ μίαν.
6 οὐ γὰρ ᾔδει τί ἀποκριθῇ,
ἔκφοβοι γὰρ ἐγένοντο.

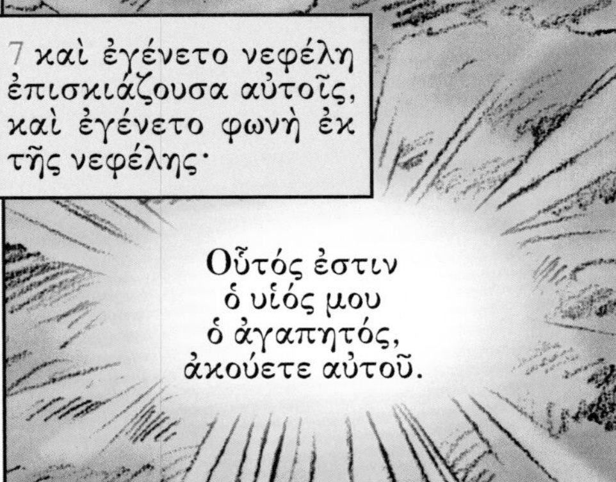
7 καὶ ἐγένετο νεφέλη
ἐπισκιάζουσα αὐτοῖς,
καὶ ἐγένετο φωνὴ ἐκ
τῆς νεφέλης·
Οὗτός ἐστιν
ὁ υἱός μου
ὁ ἀγαπητός,
ἀκούετε αὐτοῦ.

8 καὶ ἐξάπινα περιβλε-
ψάμενοι οὐκέτι οὐδένα
εἶδον ἀλλὰ τὸν Ἰησοῦν
μόνον μεθ᾽ ἑαυτῶν.

9 Καὶ καταβαινόντων
αὐτῶν ἐκ τοῦ ὄρους διε-
στείλατο αὐτοῖς ἵνα
μηδενὶ ἃ εἶδον διηγή-
σωνται, εἰ μὴ ὅταν ὁ
υἱὸς τοῦ ἀνθρώπου ἐκ
νεκρῶν ἀναστῇ.
10 καὶ τὸν λόγον ἐκρά-
τησαν πρὸς ἑαυτοὺς συ-
ζητοῦντες τί ἐστιν τὸ
ἐκ νεκρῶν ἀναστῆναι.

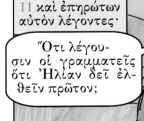

11 καὶ ἐπηρώτων
αὐτὸν λέγοντες·
Ὅτι λέγου-
σιν οἱ γραμματεῖς
ὅτι Ἠλίαν δεῖ ἐλ-
θεῖν πρῶτον;
12 ὁ δὲ ἔφη αὐτοῖς·
Ἠλίας μὲν ἐλθὼν πρῶτον ἀπο-
καθιστάνει πάντα, καὶ πῶς γέγραπται ἐπὶ τὸν υἱὸν τοῦ ἀνθρώπου ἵνα
πολλὰ πάθῃ καὶ ἐξουδενηθῇ;
13 ἀλλὰ λέγω ὑμῖν ὅτι καὶ Ἠλίας
ἐλήλυθεν, καὶ ἐποίησαν αὐτῷ ὅσα
ἤθελον, καθὼς γέγραπται ἐπ᾽ αὐτόν.

2 And after six days Jesus takes Peter and Jacob and John, and brings them alone up onto a high mountain in private. And he was transformed before them, 3 and his outer
garments became radiant, exceedingly white, such that a person cleaning clothes is not able on earth to so whiten *anything*! 4 And Elijah with Moses appeared to them,
and they were talking together with Jesus. 5 And, answering back, Peter says to Jesus, “Rabbi, it is good that we are here, and let us make three tents, one for you and one
for Moses and one for Elijah.” 6 For he had not known what he should answer back, for they became very afraid. 7 And a cloud came overshadowing them, and a voice
came from the cloud, “This is my beloved Son, keep listening to him!” 8 And unexpectedly, after looking around, no longer did they see anyone but only Jesus amongst
themselves. 9 And, while they were coming down from the mountain, he commanded them that to no one should they relate what they saw, except whenever the Son of
Man will be is raised from the dead. 10 And they held onto the matter, discussing with themselves what it is to be raised up from the dead. 11 And they kept questioning
him saying this: “Are the scribes saying that Elijah must come first?” 12 So, he was saying to them, “Elijah indeed, after coming first, reestablishes all things, and how has
it been written about the Son of Man in order that he would suffer many things and be treated with contempt? 13 But I am saying to you that also Elijah has come, and they
did to him how much they were wanting, just as it has been written regarding him.”

14 Καὶ ἐλθόντες πρὸς τοὺς μαθητὰς εἶδον ὄχλον πολὺν περὶ αὐτοὺς καὶ γραμματεῖς συζητοῦντας πρὸς αὐτούς. 15 καὶ εὐθὺς πᾶς ὁ ὄχλος ἰδόντες αὐτὸν ἐξεθαμβήθησαν, καὶ προστρέχοντες ἠσπάζοντο αὐτόν. 16 καὶ ἐπηρώτησεν αὐτούς·
Τί συζητεῖτε πρὸς αὐτούς;
17 καὶ ἀπεκρίθη αὐτῷ εἷς ἐκ τοῦ ὄχλου·
Διδάσκαλε, ἤνεγκα τὸν υἱόν μου πρὸς σέ, ἔχοντα πνεῦμα ἄλαλον·

18 καὶ ὅπου ἐὰν αὐτὸν καταλάβῃ ῥήσσει αὐτόν, καὶ ἀφρίζει καὶ τρίζει τοὺς ὀδόντας καὶ ξηραίνεται· καὶ εἶπα τοῖς μαθηταῖς σου ἵνα αὐτὸ ἐκβάλωσιν, καὶ οὐκ ἴσχυσαν.

19 ὁ δὲ ἀποκριθεὶς αὐτοῖς λέγει·
Ὦ γενεὰ ἄπιστος, ἕως πότε πρὸς ὑμᾶς ἔσομαι; ἕως πότε ἀνέξομαι ὑμῶν; φέρετε αὐτὸν πρός με.

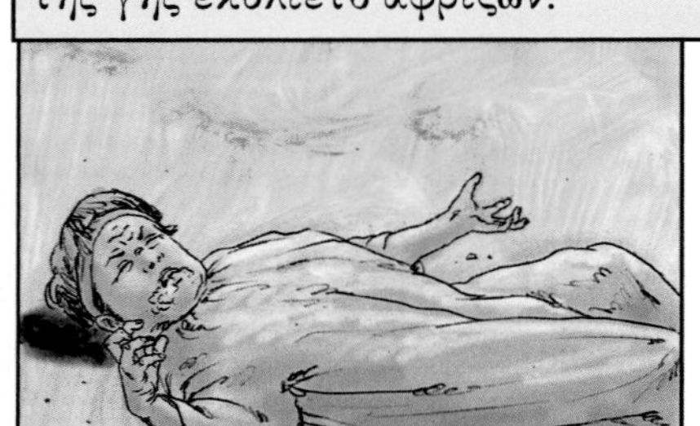
20 καὶ ἤνεγκαν αὐτὸν πρὸς αὐτόν. καὶ ἰδὼν αὐτὸν τὸ πνεῦμα εὐθὺς συνεσπάραξεν αὐτόν, καὶ πεσὼν ἐπὶ τῆς γῆς ἐκυλίετο ἀφρίζων.

21 καὶ ἐπηρώτησεν τὸν πατέρα αὐτοῦ·
Πόσος χρόνος ἐστὶν ὡς τοῦτο γέγονεν αὐτῷ;

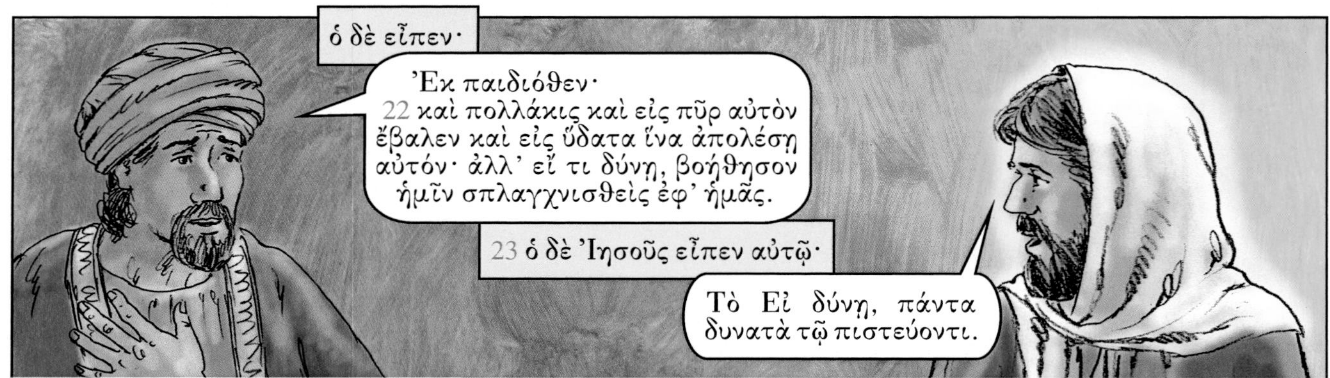
ὁ δὲ εἶπεν·
Ἐκ παιδιόθεν· 22 καὶ πολλάκις καὶ εἰς πῦρ αὐτὸν ἔβαλεν καὶ εἰς ὕδατα ἵνα ἀπολέσῃ αὐτόν· ἀλλ᾽ εἴ τι δύνῃ, βοήθησον ἡμῖν σπλαγχνισθεὶς ἐφ᾽ ἡμᾶς.
23 ὁ δὲ Ἰησοῦς εἶπεν αὐτῷ·
Τὸ Εἰ δύνῃ, πάντα δυνατὰ τῷ πιστεύοντι.

14 And after coming to the disciples, they saw a large crowd around them and scribes disputing with them. 15 And straightaway all the crowd, after seeing him, were greatly
amazed, and while running to him, they were greeting him. 16 And he asked them, "Why are you disputing with them?" 17 And one from the crowd answered back to him,
"Teacher, I brought to you my son having a mute spirit; 18 and wherever it takes him, it throws him down, and he foams at the mouth and grinds his teeth and becomes
stiff; and I spoke to your disciples in order that they would cast it out, and they were not strong enough." 19 And he, answering back, says to them, "Oh faithless generation,
how long will I be with you? How long will I put up with you? You *all* bring him to me." 20 And they brought him to him. And after seeing him, the spirit straightaway
shook him, and, after falling on the ground, he was rolling foaming at the mouth. 21 And he asked his father, "How much time is it (that) like this it has happened to him?"
Well, he said, "From childhood. 22 And many times it threw him both into the fire and into the waters in order that it would kill him; but, if in some way you are able, help
us, *by* having compassion upon us!" 23 So, Jesus said to him, "About the 'if you are able,' all things are possible for the one believing."

24 εὐθὺς κράξας ὁ πατὴρ τοῦ παιδίου ἔλεγεν·
Πιστεύω· βοήθει μου τῇ ἀπιστίᾳ.
25 ἰδὼν δὲ ὁ Ἰησοῦς ὅτι ἐπισυντρέχει ὄχλος ἐπετίμησεν τῷ πνεύματι τῷ ἀκαθάρτῳ λέγων αὐτῷ·
Τὸ ἄλαλον καὶ κωφὸν πνεῦμα, ἐγὼ ἐπιτάσσω σοι, ἔξελθε ἐξ αὐτοῦ καὶ μηκέτι εἰσέλθῃς εἰς αὐτόν.

26 καὶ κράξας καὶ πολλὰ σπαράξας ἐξῆλθεν·

καὶ ἐγένετο ὡσεὶ νεκρὸς ὥστε τοὺς πολλοὺς λέγειν ὅτι

ἀπέθανεν.

27 ὁ δὲ Ἰησοῦς κρατήσας τῆς χειρὸς αὐτοῦ ἤγειρεν αὐτόν, καὶ ἀνέστη.

28 καὶ εἰσελθόν-τος αὐτοῦ εἰς οἶκ-ον οἱ μαθηταὶ αὐτοῦ κατ' ἰδίαν ἐπηρώτων αὐτόν·
Ὅτι ἡμεῖς οὐκ ἠδυνήθημεν ἐκβαλεῖν αὐτό;
29 καὶ εἶπεν αὐτοῖς·
Τοῦτο τὸ γένος ἐν οὐδενὶ δύναται ἐξελθεῖν εἰ μὴ ἐν προσευχῇ.

30 Κἀκεῖθεν ἐξελθόντες παρεπορεύοντο διὰ τῆς Γαλιλαίας, καὶ οὐκ ἤθελεν ἵνα τις γνοῖ·
31 ἐδίδασκεν γὰρ τοὺς μαθητὰς αὐτοῦ καὶ ἔλεγεν αὐτοῖς ὅτι
Ὁ υἱὸς τοῦ ἀνθρώπου παραδίδοται εἰς χεῖρας ἀνθρώπων, καὶ ἀποκτενοῦσιν αὐτόν, καὶ ἀποκτανθεὶς μετὰ τρεῖς ἡμέρας ἀναστήσεται.
32 οἱ δὲ ἠγνόουν τὸ ῥῆμα, καὶ ἐφοβοῦντο αὐτὸν ἐπερωτῆσαι.
33 Καὶ ἦλθον εἰς Καφαρναουμ.

24 Shouting immediately, the father of the child was saying, "I believe! Help my disbelief!" 25 Well, after Jesus saw that a crowd was running together, he rebuked the
unclean spirit saying to it, "You mute and deaf spirit, I myself command you, come out from him and no longer enter into him!" 26 And after shouting and shaking him
much, it came out; and he became like a dead person, so that many were saying that he had died. 27 Well, Jesus, after seizing his hand, raised him up, and he arose. 28 And
after he entered into a house, his disciples were asking him in private, "Why were we ourselves not able to cast it out?" 29 And he said to them, "This very kind in no way
is able to come out except in prayer." 30 And after going out from there, they were passing through Galilee, and he was not wanting that anyone know. 31 For he was
teaching his disciples and was saying to them this: "The Son of Man is being delivered over into the hands of people, and they will kill him, and, after being killed, after
three days he will rise again." 32 But they were not comprehending the saying, and they were fearing to ask him. 33 And they came into Capernaum.

κα ν τῇ ο κ ᾳ γενόμενος ἐπηρώτα αὐτούς·
Τί ἐν τῇ ὁδῷ διελογίζεσθε;
34 οἱ δὲ ἐσιώπων, πρὸς ἀλλήλους γὰρ διελέχθησαν ἐν τῇ ὁδῷ τίς μείζων.

καὶ καθίσας ἐφώνησεν τοὺς δώδεκα καὶ λέγει αὐτοῖς·
Εἴ τις θέλει πρῶτος εἶναι ἔσται πάντων ἔσχατος καὶ πάντων διάκονος.

36 καὶ λαβὼν παιδίον ἔστησεν αὐτὸ ἐν μέσῳ αὐτῶν καὶ ἐναγκαλισάμενος αὐτὸ εἶπεν αὐτοῖς·

37 Ὃς ἂν ἓν τῶν τοιούτων παιδίων δέξηται ἐπὶ τῷ ὀνόματί μου, ἐμὲ δέχεται· καὶ ὃς ⸀ἂν ἐμὲ δέχηται, οὐκ ἐμὲ δέχεται ἀλλὰ τὸν ἀποστείλαντά με.

38 Ἔφη αὐτῷ ὁ Ἰωάννης·
Διδάσκαλε, εἴδομέν τινα ἐν τῷ ὀνόματί σου ἐκβάλλοντα δαιμόνια, καὶ ἐκωλύομεν αὐτόν, ὅτι οὐκ ἠκολούθει ἡμῖν.

39 ὁ δὲ Ἰησοῦς εἶπεν·
Μὴ κωλύετε αὐτόν, οὐδεὶς γάρ ἐστιν ὃς ποιήσει δύναμιν ἐπὶ τῷ ὀνόματί μου καὶ δυνήσεται ταχὺ κακολογῆσαί με· 40 ὃς γὰρ οὐκ ἔστιν καθ’ ἡμῶν, ὑπὲρ ἡμῶν ἐστιν. 41 Ὃς γὰρ ἂν ποτίσῃ ὑμᾶς ποτήριον ὕδατος ἐν ὀνόματι ὅτι χριστοῦ ἐστε, ἀμὴν λέγω ὑμῖν ὅτι οὐ μὴ ἀπολέσῃ τὸν μισθὸν αὐτοῦ.

42 Καὶ ὃς ἂν σκανδαλίσῃ ἕνα τῶν μικρῶν τούτων τῶν πιστευόντων εἰς ἐμέ, καλόν ἐστιν αὐτῷ μᾶλλον εἰ περίκειται μύλος ὀνικὸς περὶ τὸν τράχηλον αὐτοῦ καὶ βέβληται εἰς τὴν θάλασσαν.
43 Καὶ ἐὰν σκανδαλίζῃ σε ἡ χείρ σου, ἀπόκοψον αὐτήν· καλόν ἐστίν σε κυλλὸν εἰσελθεῖν εἰς τὴν ζωὴν ἢ τὰς δύο χεῖρας ἔχοντα ἀπελθεῖν εἰς τὴν γέενναν, εἰς τὸ πῦρ τὸ ἄσβεστον. 44 [ὅπου ὁ σκώληξ αὐτῶν οὐ τελευτᾷ, καὶ τὸ πῦρ οὐ σβέννυται.]

And after coming in the house, he was asking them, "What were you debating on the way?" 34 But they were being quiet, for they argued with one another on the way
about who *was* the greatest. 35 And after sitting down, he called the twelve and he begins saying to them, "If someone wants to be first, he shall be last of all and servant
of all." 36 And, after taking a little child, he set the child in the middle of them, and after hugging the child, he said to them, 37 "Whoever receives one of such little children
as these in my name, receives me; and whoever receives me, does not receive me but the one who sent me." 38 John was saying to him, "Teacher, we saw someone in your
name casting out demons, and we were forbidding him, because he was not following us." 39 So, Jesus said, "You *all* do not go on forbidding him! For there is no one who
will perform a miracle in my name and be able immediately to speak evil of me. 40 For whoever is not against us, is for us. 41 For whoever gives you a cup of water in *my*
name because you are Christ's - Amen! - I am saying to you that he will never ever lose his reward. 42 And whoever causes one of these little ones believing in me to
stumble, it is better for him rather if a large millstone is hung around his neck and he has been thrown into the sea. 43 And, if your hand causes you to stumble, cut it off!
It is better for you to enter into life maimed than, having your two hands, to go into Gehenna, into the unquenchable fire, 44 *where their worm does not die, and the fire is
not being extinguished.*

κα ν πο ς σου σκαν-
δαλίζῃ σε, ἀπόκοψον αὐτόν·
καλόν ἐστίν σε εἰσελθεῖν εἰς
τὴν ζωὴν χωλὸν ἢ τοὺς δύο
πόδας ἔχοντα βληθῆναι εἰς τὴν
γέενναν.
46 [ὅπου ὁ σκώληξ αὐτῶν οὐ
τελευτᾷ, καὶ τὸ πῦρ οὐ σβέννυται.
47 καὶ ἐὰν ὁ ὀφθαλμός σου
σκανδαλίζῃ σε, ἔκβαλε αὐτόν·
καλόν σέ ἐστιν μονόφθαλμον
εἰσελθεῖν εἰς τὴν βασιλείαν τοῦ
θεοῦ ἢ δύο ὀφθαλμοὺς ἔχοντα
βληθῆναι εἰς τὴν γέενναν,
48 ὅπου ὁ σκώληξ αὐτῶν οὐ τε-
ευτ κα τ π ρ ο σ ννυ-
ται.
49 Πᾶς γὰρ πυρὶ ἁλισθήσεται.
50 καλὸν τὸ ἅλας· ἐὰν δὲ τὸ
ἅλας ἄναλον γένηται, ἐν τίνι
αὐτὸ ἀρτύσετε; ἔχετε ἐν ἑαυτοῖς
ἅλα, καὶ εἰρηνεύετε ἐν ἀλλή-
λοις.

Κεφ.
ΙΑ´

1 Καὶ ἐκεῖθεν ἀναστὰς
ἔρχεται εἰς τὰ ὅρια τῆς
Ἰουδαίας καὶ πέραν
τοῦ Ἰορδάνου, καὶ συμ-
πορεύονται πάλιν ὄχ-
λοι πρὸς αὐτόν, καὶ ὡς
εἰώθει πάλιν ἐδίδασ-
κεν αὐτούς.

2 Καὶ ἐπηρώτων αὐτὸν εἰ ἔξεστιν ἀνδρὶ γυναῖκα ἀπολῦσαι, πειράζοντες αὐτόν.
3 ὁ δὲ ἀποκριθεὶς εἶπεν αὐτοῖς·
Τί ὑμῖν ἐνετείλατο Μωϋσῆς;
4 οἱ δὲ εἶπαν·
Ἐπέτρεψεν Μωϋσῆς βιβλίον ἀποστασίου γράψαι καὶ ἀπολῦσαι.

45 And, if your foot causes you to stumble, cut it off! It is better for you to enter into life maimed than, having your two feet, to go into Gehenna, 46 *where their worm does*
not die, and the fire is not being extinguished. 47 And, if your eye causes you to stumble, cast it out! It is better for you to enter into the Kingdom of God one-eyed than,
having two eyes, to go into Gehenna; 48 where their worm does not die and the fire is not being extinguished. 49 For everyone will be salted with fire. 50 Salt is good; but if
the salt becomes unsalty, in what will you *all* prepare it? Have salt in yourselves! And be at peace one with another!" 10:1 And after arising from there, he comes to the
region of Judaea and beyond the Jordan, and again the crowds go together to him, and, as was customary, again he was teaching them. 2 And they began asking him if it
was allowed for a husband to divorce a wife, testing him. 3 But he, answering back, said to them, "What did Moses command you?" 4 And they said, "Moses permitted to
write a certificate of divorce and to divorce."

5 ὁ δὲ Ἰησοῦς εἶπεν αὐτοῖς·
Πρὸς τὴν σκληροκαρδίαν ὑμῶν ἔγραψεν ὑμῖν τὴν ἐντολὴν ταύτην·
6 ἀπὸ δὲ ἀρχῆς κτίσεως ἄρσεν καὶ θῆλυ ἐποίησεν αὐτούς·
7 ἕνεκεν τούτου καταλείψει ἄνθρωπος τὸν πατέρα αὐτοῦ καὶ τὴν μητέρα καὶ προσκολληθήσεται πρὸς τὴν γυναῖκα αὐτοῦ,
8 καὶ ἔσονται οἱ δύο εἰς σάρκα μίαν· ὥστε οὐκέτι εἰσὶν δύο ἀλλὰ μία σάρξ·
9 ὃ οὖν ὁ θεὸς συνέζευξεν ἄνθρωπος μὴ χωριζέτω

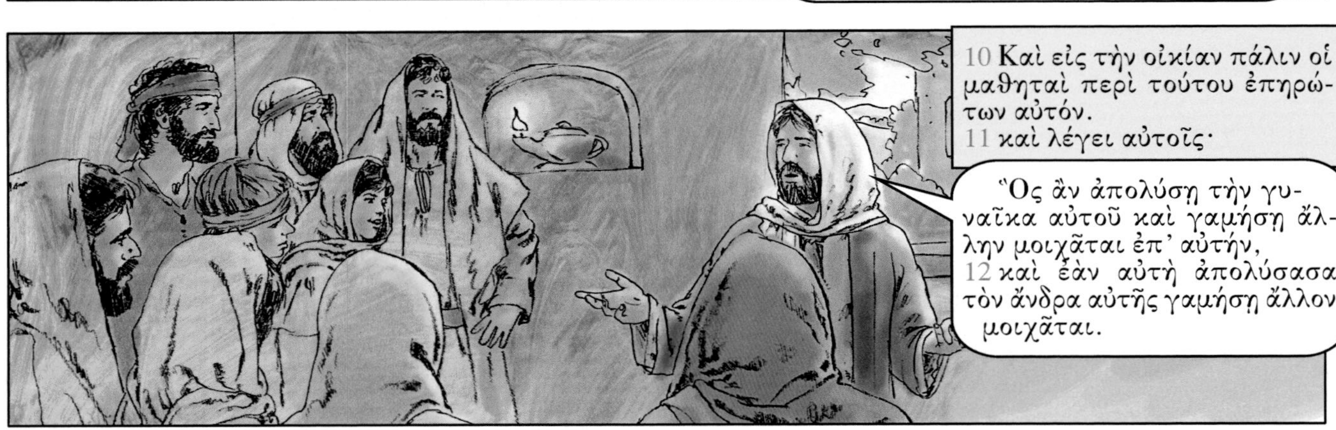
10 Καὶ εἰς τὴν οἰκίαν πάλιν οἱ μαθηταὶ περὶ τούτου ἐπηρώτων αὐτόν.
11 καὶ λέγει αὐτοῖς·
Ὃς ἂν ἀπολύσῃ τὴν γυναῖκα αὐτοῦ καὶ γαμήσῃ ἄλλην μοιχᾶται ἐπ᾽ αὐτήν,
12 καὶ ἐὰν αὐτὴ ἀπολύσασα τὸν ἄνδρα αὐτῆς γαμήσῃ ἄλλον μοιχᾶται.

13 Καὶ προσέφερον αὐτῷ παιδία ἵνα αὐτῶν ἅψηται· οἱ δὲ μαθηταὶ ἐπετίμησαν αὐτοῖς.
14 ἰδὼν δὲ ὁ Ἰησοῦς ἠγανάκτησεν καὶ εἶπεν αὐτοῖς·
Ἄφετε τὰ παιδία ἔρχεσθαι πρός με, μὴ κωλύετε αὐτά, τῶν γὰρ τοιούτων ἐστὶν ἡ βασιλεία τοῦ θεοῦ.
15 ἀμὴν λέγω ὑμῖν, ὃς ἂν μὴ δέξηται τὴν βασιλείαν τοῦ θεοῦ ὡς παιδίον, οὐ μὴ εἰσέλθῃ εἰς αὐτήν.
16 καὶ ἐναγκαλισάμενος αὐτὰ κατευλόγει τιθεὶς τὰς χεῖρας ἐπ᾽ αὐτά.

[5] But Jesus said to them, "In consequence of your hard heart he wrote for you this commandment. [6] But from the beginning of creation male and female he made them.
[7] On account of this, a person will leave his father and his mother and will be joined to his wife, [8] and the two will become one flesh; so that no longer are they two but
one flesh. [9] Therefore, that which God joined together let no person separate." [10] And into the house, again, the disciples kept asking him about this. [11] And he says to them,
"Whoever divorces his wife and marries another is committing adultery against her, [12] and, if she herself, after divorcing her husband, marries another, she commits
adultery." [13] And they were carrying to him little children in order that he would touch them; but the disciples rebuked them. [14] Well, after seeing, Jesus was indignant and
said to them, "Permit the little children to come to me! Do not hinder them, because the Kingdom of God belongs to ones such as these! [15] Amen! I am saying to you,
whoever does not receive the Kingdom of God as a little child will never ever enter it." [16] And, after hugging them, he was blessing *them* by laying his hands upon them.

17 Καὶ ἐκπορευομένου αὐτοῦ εἰς ὁδὸν προσδραμὼν εἷς καὶ γονυπετήσας αὐτὸν ἐπηρώτα αὐτόν·
Διδάσκαλε ἀγαθέ, τί ποιήσω ἵνα ζωὴν αἰώνιον κληρονομήσω;
Τί με λέγεις ἀγαθόν; οὐδεὶς ἀγαθὸς εἰ μὴ εἷς ὁ θεός.
19 τὰς ἐντολὰς οἶδας·
Μὴ φονεύσης,
Μὴ μοιχεύσης,
Μὴ κλέψης,
Μὴ ψευδομαρτυρήσης,
Μὴ ἀποστερήσης,
Τίμα τὸν πατέρα σου καὶ τὴν μητέρα.

20 ὁ δὲ ἔφη αὐτῷ·
Διδάσκαλε, ταῦτα πάντα ἐφυλαξάμην ἐκ νεότητός μου.

21 ὁ δὲ Ἰησοῦς ἐμβλέψας αὐτῷ ἠγάπησεν αὐτὸν καὶ εἶπεν αὐτῷ·
Ἕν σε ὑστερεῖ· ὕπαγε ὅσα ἔχεις πώλησον καὶ δὸς τοῖς πτωχοῖς, καὶ ἕξεις θησαυρὸν ἐν οὐρανῷ, καὶ δεῦρο ἀκολούθει μοι.
22 ὁ δὲ στυγνάσας ἐπὶ τῷ λόγῳ ἀπῆλθεν λυπούμενος, ἦν γὰρ ἔχων κτήματα πολλά.

23 Καὶ περιβλεψάμενος ὁ Ἰησοῦς λέγει τοῖς μαθηταῖς αὐτοῦ·
Πῶς δυσκόλως οἱ τὰ χρήματα ἔχοντες εἰς τὴν βασιλείαν τοῦ θεοῦ εἰσελεύσονται.

24 οἱ δὲ μαθηταὶ ἐθαμβοῦντο ἐπὶ τοῖς λόγοις αὐτοῦ. ὁ δὲ Ἰησοῦς πάλιν ἀποκριθεὶς λέγει αὐτοῖς·
Τέκνα, πῶς δύσκολόν ἐστιν εἰς τὴν βασιλείαν τοῦ θεοῦ εἰσελθεῖν·

25 εὐκοπώτερόν ἐστιν κάμηλον διὰ τῆς τρυμαλιᾶς τῆς ῥαφίδος διελθεῖν ἢ πλούσιον εἰς τὴν βασιλείαν τοῦ θεοῦ εἰσελθεῖν.

26 οἱ δὲ περισσῶς ἐξεπλήσσοντο λέγοντες πρὸς ἑαυτούς·
Καὶ τίς δύναται σωθῆναι;

27 ἐμβλέψας αὐτοῖς ὁ Ἰησοῦς λέγει·
Παρὰ ἀνθρώποις ἀδύνατον ἀλλ' οὐ παρὰ θεῷ, πάντα γὰρ δυνατὰ παρὰ τῷ θεῷ.

[17] And, while he was going out on the way, one man running up and kneeling before him was asking him, "Good Teacher, what shall I do in order that I would inherit
eternal life?" [18] So, Jesus said to him, "Why are calling me good? No one is good except one, *namely*, God. [19] You know the commandments: "Do not kill, Do not commit
adultery, Do not steal, Do not bear false witness, Do not defraud, Honor your father and mother." [20] But he was saying to him, "Teacher, all these things I have observed
from my youth." [21] Well, Jesus, after looking upon him, loved him and said to him, "One thing is lacking from you: Go. As much as you have, sell and give to the poor,
and you will have treasure in heaven, and come here, follow me!" [22] But he, shocked at the word, departed grieving, for he was having many possessions. [23] And, after
looking around, Jesus says to his disciples, "How the ones having possessions will enter into the Kingdom of God with difficulty!" [24] Well, the disciples were marveling
at his words. But Jesus, again answering back, says to them, "Children, how difficult it is to enter into the Kingdom of God! [25] It is easier for a camel to go through the
hole of a needle than for a rich man to enter into the Kingdom of God." [26] But they were exceedingly being astonished, saying to themselves, "Who even is able to be
saved?" [27] After looking at them, Jesus says, "With people *it is* impossible but not with God, for all things *are* possible with God."

28 ρ ατο λ γειν ὁ Πέτρος αὐτῷ·
Ἰδοὺ ἡμεῖς ἀφήκαμεν πάντα καὶ ἠκολουθήκαμέν σοι.
29 ἔφη ὁ Ἰησοῦς·
Ἀμὴν λέγω ὑμῖν, οὐδείς ἐστιν ὃς ἀφῆκεν οἰκίαν ἢ ἀδελφοὺς ἢ ἀδελφὰς ἢ μητέρα ἢ πατέρα ἢ τέκνα ἢ ἀγροὺς ἕνεκεν ἐμοῦ καὶ ἕνεκεν τοῦ εὐαγγελίου,
30 ἐὰν μὴ λάβῃ ἑκατονταπλασίονα νῦν ἐν τῷ καιρῷ τούτῳ οἰκίας καὶ ἀδελφοὺς καὶ ἀδελφὰς καὶ μητέρας καὶ τέκνα καὶ ἀγροὺς μετὰ διωγμῶν, καὶ ἐν τῷ αἰῶνι τῷ ἐρχομένῳ ζωὴν αἰώνιον.

31 πολλοὶ δὲ ἔσονται πρῶτοι ἔσχατοι καὶ οἱ ἔσχατοι πρῶτοι.
32 Ἦσαν δὲ ἐν τῇ ὁδῷ ἀναβαίνοντες εἰς Ἱεροσόλυμα, καὶ ἦν προάγων αὐτοὺς ὁ Ἰησοῦς, καὶ ἐθαμβοῦντο, οἱ δὲ ἀκολουθοῦντες ἐφοβοῦντο.

καὶ παραλαβὼν πάλιν τοὺς δώδεκα ἤρξατο αὐτοῖς λέγειν τὰ μέλλοντα αὐτῷ συμβαίνειν 33 ὅτι
Ἰδοὺ ἀναβαίνομεν εἰς Ἱεροσόλυμα, καὶ ὁ υἱὸς τοῦ ἀνθρώπου παραδοθήσεται τοῖς ἀρχιερεῦσιν καὶ τοῖς γραμματεῦσιν, καὶ κατακρινοῦσιν αὐτὸν θανάτῳ καὶ παραδώσουσιν αὐτὸν τοῖς ἔθνεσιν
34 καὶ ἐμπαίξουσιν αὐτῷ καὶ ἐμπτύσουσιν αὐτῷ καὶ μαστιγώσουσιν αὐτὸν καὶ ἀποκτενοῦσιν, καὶ μετὰ τρεῖς ἡμέρας ἀναστήσεται.

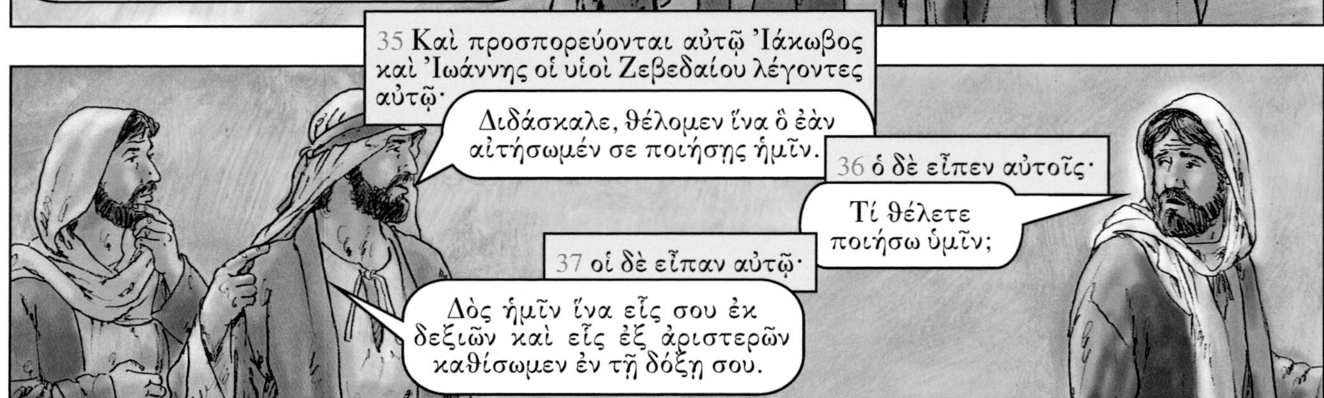
35 Καὶ προσπορεύονται αὐτῷ Ἰάκωβος καὶ Ἰωάννης οἱ υἱοὶ Ζεβεδαίου λέγοντες αὐτῷ·
Διδάσκαλε, θέλομεν ἵνα ὃ ἐὰν αἰτήσωμέν σε ποιήσῃς ἡμῖν.
36 ὁ δὲ εἶπεν αὐτοῖς·
Τί θέλετε ποιήσω ὑμῖν;
37 οἱ δὲ εἶπαν αὐτῷ·
Δὸς ἡμῖν ἵνα εἷς σου ἐκ δεξιῶν καὶ εἷς ἐξ ἀριστερῶν καθίσωμεν ἐν τῇ δόξῃ σου.

[28] Peter began to say to him, "Look, we ourselves abandoned all things and have followed you." [29] Jesus was saying, "Amen! I am saying to you *all*, there is no one who
abandoned household or brothers or sisters or mother or father or children or lands on account of me and on account of the gospel, [30] except he receives a hundredfold now
in this time, houses and brothers and sisters and mothers and children and lands with persecutions, and, in the age to come, everlasting life. [31] But many first ones will be
last and the last first." [32] Well, they were on the way going up into Jerusalem, and Jesus was leading them, and they were marveling, but the ones following were being
afraid. And after taking aside again the Twelve, he began to say to them the things about to happen to him, [33] *namely,* this: "Behold, we are going up into Jerusalem, and
the Son of Man will be handed over to the chief priests and to the scribes, and they will condemn him to death and they will hand him over to the Gentiles, [34] and they will
mock him and they will spit upon him and will scourge him and will kill him, and after three days he will arise. [35] And they come near to him, James and John, the sons
of Zebedee, saying to him, "Teacher, we want that, whatever we ask you, you would do for us." [36] Well, he said to them, "What do you want that I should do for you?"
[37] So, they said to him, "Grant to us that we, one on the right and one on the left, would sit in your glory."

38 ὁ δὲ Ἰησοῦς εἶπεν αὐτοῖς·
Οὐκ οἴδατε τί αἰτεῖσθε· δύνασθε πιεῖν τὸ ποτήριον ὃ ἐγὼ πίνω, ἢ τὸ βάπτισμα ὃ ἐγὼ βαπτίζομαι βαπτισθῆναι;
39 οἱ δὲ εἶπαν αὐτῷ·
Δυνάμεθα.
ὁ δὲ Ἰησοῦς εἶπεν αὐτοῖς·
Τὸ ποτήριον ὃ ἐγὼ πίνω πίεσθε καὶ τὸ βάπτισμα ὃ ἐγὼ βαπτίζομαι βαπτισθήσεσθε,

40 τὸ δὲ καθίσαι ἐκ δεξιῶν μου ἢ ἐξ εὐωνύμων οὐκ ἔστιν ἐμὸν δοῦναι, ἀλλ᾽ οἷς ἡτοίμασται.
41 Καὶ ἀκούσαντες οἱ δέκα ἤρξαντο ἀγανακτεῖν περὶ Ἰακώβου καὶ Ἰωάννου.
42 καὶ προσκαλεσάμενος αὐτοὺς ὁ Ἰησοῦς λέγει αὐτοῖς·

Οἴδατε ὅτι οἱ δοκοῦντες ἄρχειν τῶν ἐθνῶν κατακυριεύουσιν αὐτῶν καὶ οἱ μεγάλοι αὐτῶν κατεξουσιάζουσιν αὐτῶν.
43 οὐχ οὕτως δέ ἐστιν ἐν ὑμῖν· ἀλλ᾽ ὃς ἂν θέλῃ μέγας γενέσθαι ἐν ὑμῖν, ἔσται ὑμῶν διάκονος,
44 καὶ ὃς ἂν θέλῃ ἐν ὑμῖν εἶναι πρῶτος, ἔσται πάντων δοῦλος·
45 καὶ γὰρ ὁ υἱὸς τοῦ ἀνθρώπου οὐκ ἦλθεν διακονηθῆναι ἀλλὰ διακονῆσαι καὶ δοῦναι τὴν ψυχὴν αὐτοῦ λύτρον ἀντὶ πολλῶν.

46 Καὶ ἔρχονται εἰς Ἰεριχώ. καὶ ἐκπορευομένου αὐτοῦ ἀπὸ Ἰεριχὼ καὶ τῶν μαθητῶν αὐτοῦ καὶ ὄχλου ἱκανοῦ ὁ υἱὸς Τιμαίου Βαρτιμαῖος τυφλὸς προσαίτης ἐκάθητο παρὰ τὴν ὁδόν.
47 καὶ ἀκούσας ὅτι Ἰησοῦς ὁ Ναζαρηνός ἐστιν ἤρξατο κράζειν καὶ λέγειν·
Υἱὲ Δαυὶδ Ἰησοῦ, ἐλέησόν με.
48 καὶ ἐπετίμων αὐτῷ πολλοὶ ἵνα σιωπήσῃ· ὁ δὲ πολλῷ μᾶλλον ἔκραζεν·
Υἱὲ Δαυίδ, ἐλέησόν με.

[38] Well, Jesus said to them, "You *two* do not know what you are asking. Are you able to drink the cup that I myself am drinking, or to be baptized with the baptism that I
myself am being baptized with?" [39] Well, they said to him, "We are able." So, Jesus said to them, "The cup that I myself am drinking you will drink and the baptism that
I myself am baptized with you will be baptized with, [40] but to sit on my right or on the left is not mine to give, but *it is* for those whom it has been prepared." [41] And after
hearing, the ten began to be indignant about Jacob and John. [42] And after calling them together, Jesus says to them, "You know that the ones recognized to rule over the
nations lord *it* over them and their great ones exercise authority over them. [43] Well, it is not so among you *all*; but whoever wants to become great among you will be your
servant, [44] and whoever wants to be first among you will be a servant of all. [45] For even the Son of Man did not come to be served but to serve and to give his life *to be* a
ransom for many." [46] And they come into Jericho. And, while he was leaving from Jericho and his disciples and a considerable crowd, the son of Timaeus, Bartimaeus, a
blind beggar, was sitting along the way. [47] And after hearing that it was Jesus the Nazarene, he began to cry out and to say, "Son of David, Jesus, pity me!" [48] And many
were rebuking him in order that he would be quiet; well, he much more cried out, "Son of David, pity me!"

49 καὶ στὰς ὁ Ἰησοῦς εἶπεν·
Φωνήσατε αὐτόν.

κα φωνοῦσι τ ν τυφ-λὸν λέγοντες αὐτῷ·
Θάρσει, ἔγειρε, φωνεῖ σε.

50 ὁ δὲ ἀποβαλὼν τὸ ἱμάτιον αὐτοῦ ἀναπηδήσας ἦλθεν πρὸς τὸν Ἰησοῦν.

51 καὶ ἀποκριθεὶς αὐ-τῷ ὁ Ἰησοῦς εἶπεν·
Τί σοι θέ-λεις ποιήσω;
ὁ δὲ τυφλὸς εἶπεν αὐτῷ·
Ραββουνι, ἵνα ἀναβλέψω.

52 καὶ ὁ Ἰησοῦς εἶπεν αὐτῷ·
Ὕπαγε, ἡ πίστις σου σέσωκέν σε.

καὶ εὐθὺς ἀνέβλεψεν, καὶ ἠκολούθει αὐτῷ ἐν τῇ ὁδῷ.

Κεφ.
ΙΒ´

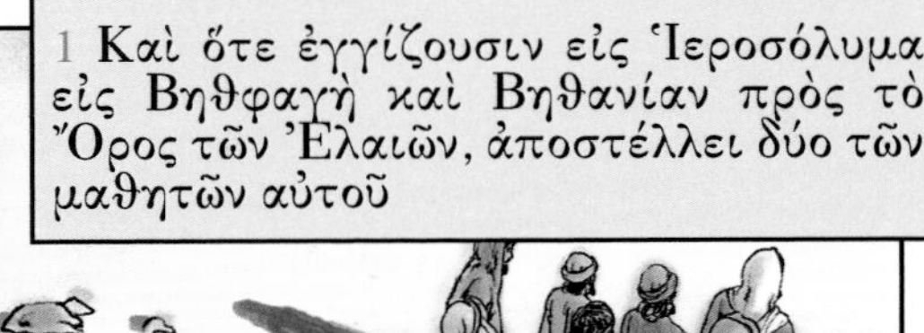
1 Καὶ ὅτε ἐγγίζουσιν εἰς Ἱεροσόλυμα εἰς Βηθφαγὴ καὶ Βηθανίαν πρὸς τὸ Ὄρος τῶν Ἐλαιῶν, ἀποστέλλει δύο τῶν μαθητῶν αὐτοῦ

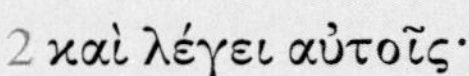
2 καὶ λέγει αὐτοῖς·

Ὑπάγετε εἰς τὴν κώμην τὴν κατέναντι ὑμῶν, καὶ εὐθὺς εἰσπορευόμενοι εἰς αὐτὴν εὑρήσετε πῶλον δεδεμένον ἐφ' ὃν οὐδεὶς οὔπω ἀνθρώπων ἐκάθισεν· λύσατε αὐτὸν καὶ φέρετε. 3 καὶ ἐάν τις ὑμῖν εἴπῃ· Τί ποιεῖτε τοῦτο; εἴπατε ὅτι Ὁ κύριος αὐτοῦ χρείαν ἔχει· καὶ εὐθὺς αὐτὸν ἀποστέλλει πάλιν ὧδε.

4 καὶ ἀπῆλθον καὶ εὗρον πῶλον δεδεμένον πρὸς θύραν ἔξω ἐπὶ τοῦ ἀμφόδου, καὶ λύουσιν αὐτόν.

49 And, after standing, Jesus said, "You *all* call him!" And they call the blind man saying to him, "Have courage! Rise up! He calls you." 50 Well, he, after throwing off his
outer garment springing up, came to Jesus. 51 And answering back to him, Jesus said, "What do you want me to do for you?" So, the blind man said to him, "Teacher, that
I would see again." 52 And Jesus said to him, "Go, your faith has restored you." And straightaway he received sight, and he was following him on the way. 11:1 And when
they are drawing near into Jerusalem, into Bethphage and Bethany, before the Mount of Olives, he sends two of his disciples, 2 and he begins saying to them, "Go into the
village before you, and straightaway while entering it, you will find a colt having been tied up, upon which no person has ever sat; untie and bring it. 3 And if someone
says to you, 'Why are you doing this?' say this: ''The Lord has need of it; and straightaway he will send it again here.'" 4 And they went away and found a colt having
been tied in front of the door outside on the street, and they begin untying it.

5 καὶ τινες τῶν ἐκεῖ ἑστη-
κότων ἔλεγον αὐτοῖς·
Τί ποιεῖτε
λύοντες τὸν
πῶλον;

6 οἱ δὲ εἶπαν αὐτοῖς
καθὼς εἶπεν ὁ Ἰησοῦς·
καὶ ἀφῆκαν αὐτούς.
7 καὶ φέρουσιν τὸν πῶ-
λον πρὸς τὸν Ἰησοῦν,
καὶ ἐπιβάλλουσιν αὐτῷ
τὰ ἱμάτια αὐτῶν, καὶ
ἐκάθισεν ἐπ᾽ αὐτόν.

8 καὶ πολλοὶ τὰ ἱμάτια αὐτῶν
ἔστρωσαν εἰς τὴν ὁδόν, ἄλλοι δὲ
στιβάδας κόψαντες ἐκ τῶν ἀγρῶν.
9 καὶ οἱ προάγοντες καὶ οἱ ἀκολουθοῦντες ἔκραζον·

Ὡσαννά·

Εὐλογημένος ὁ ἐρχόμενος ἐν ὀνόματι κυρίου·

10 Εὐλογημένη ἡ ἐρχομένη βασιλεία τοῦ πατρὸς ἡμῶν Δαυίδ· Ὡσαννὰ ἐν τοῖς ὑψίστοις.

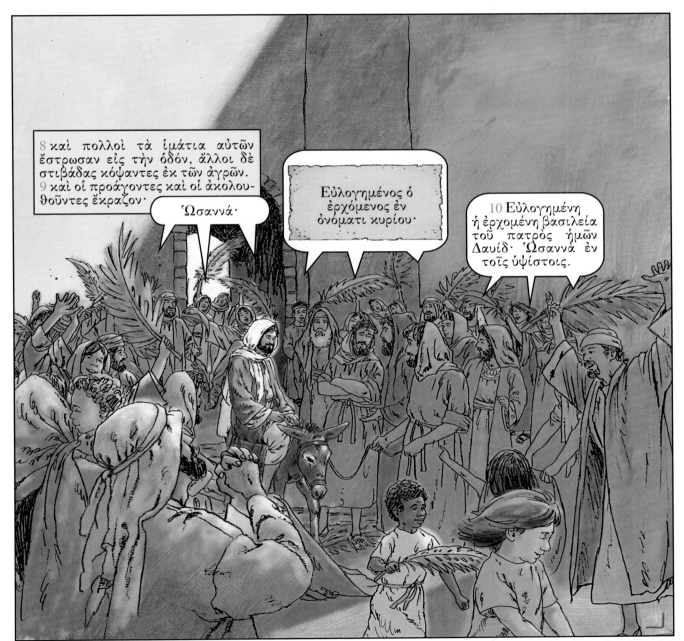

5 And some of the ones standing there were saying to them, "What are you doing untying the colt?" 6 So, they said to them just as Jesus said; and they released them. 7 And
they bring the colt to Jesus, and they throw their outer garments upon it, and he sat upon it. 8 And many people spread their outer garments onto the road, but others *were*
cutting branches from the fields. 9 And the ones going before and the ones following were crying out, "Hosanna! Blessed is the one coming in the name of the Lord!
10 Blessed is the coming kingdom of our father David! Hosanna in the highest!"

11 Καὶ εἰσῆλθεν
εἰς Ἱεροσόλυμα
εἰς τὸ ἱερόν·

καὶ περιβλεψάμενος πάντα ὀψὲ ἤδη
οὔσης τῆς ὥρας ἐξῆλθεν εἰς Βηθανίαν
μετὰ τῶν δώδεκα.

12 Καὶ τῇ ἐπαύριον ἐξελ-
θόντων αὐτῶν ἀπὸ Βηθα-
νίας ἐπείνασεν.
13 καὶ ἰδὼν συκῆν ἀπὸ μα-
κρόθεν ἔχουσαν φύλλα ἦλ-
θεν εἰ ἄρα τι εὑρήσει ἐν
αὐτῇ, καὶ ἐλθὼν ἐπ᾽ αὐτὴν
οὐδὲν εὗρεν εἰ μὴ φύλλα, ὁ
γὰρ καιρὸς οὐκ ἦν σύκων.
14 καὶ ἀποκριθεὶς εἶπεν
αὐτῇ·
Μηκέτι εἰς τὸν αἰῶνα ἐκ
σοῦ μηδεὶς καρπὸν φάγοι.
καὶ ἤκουον οἱ
μαθηταὶ αὐτοῦ.

15 Καὶ ἔρχονται εἰς
Ἱεροσόλυμα. καὶ εἰσελ-
θὼν εἰς τὸ ἱερὸν ἤρξατο
ἐκβάλλειν τοὺς πωλοῦν-
τας καὶ τοὺς ἀγοράζον-
τας ἐν τῷ ἱερῷ, καὶ τὰς
τραπέζας τῶν κολλυ-
βισ-τῶν καὶ τὰς καθέ-
δρας τῶν πωλούντων τὰς
περιστερὰς κατέστρε-
ψεν
16 καὶ οὐκ ἤφιεν ἵνα τις
διενέγκῃ σκεῦος διὰ
τοῦ ἱεροῦ,
17 καὶ ἐδίδασκεν καὶ
ἔλεγεν αὐτοῖς·
Οὐ γέγραπται ὅτι
Ὁ οἶκός μου οἶκος
προσευχῆς κληθήσεται
πᾶσιν τοῖς ἔθνεσιν;
ὑμεῖς δὲ πεποιήκατε
αὐτὸν σπήλαιον λῃστῶν.

[11] And he entered into Jerusalem into the temple; and after looking around at everything, *since* the hour was already late, he went out into Bethany with the twelve. [12] And on the next day, after they came out from Bethany, he was hungry. [13] And after seeing a fig tree from afar having leaves, he went, *to see* if therefore he would find something on it; and after coming to it, he found nothing except leaves, for it was not the season of figs. [14] And responding back, he said to it, "No longer forever may anyone eat fruit from you." And his disciples were listening. [15] And they come into Jerusalem. And after entering into the temple, he began to cast out the ones selling and the ones buying in the temple, and he turned over the tables of the money-changers and the seats of the ones selling the doves; [16] and he was not allowing that someone would carry a vessel through the temple. [17] And began teaching and he was saying to them, "Hasn't it been written, 'My house will be called a house of payer for all the nations?' *Surely, yes!* But you yourselves have made it a den of bandits."

18 καὶ ἤκουσαν οἱ ἀρχιερεῖς καὶ οἱ γραμματεῖς, καὶ ἐζήτουν πῶς αὐτὸν ἀπολέσωσιν· ἐφοβοῦντο γὰρ αὐτόν, πᾶς γὰρ ὁ ὄχλος ἐξεπλήσσετο ἐπὶ τῇ διδαχῇ αὐτοῦ.

19 Καὶ ὅταν ὀψὲ ἐγένετο, ἐξεπορεύοντο ἔξω τῆς πόλεως.

20 Καὶ παραπορευόμενοι πρωῒ εἶδον τὴν συκῆν ἐξηραμμένην ἐκ ῥιζῶν.
21 καὶ ἀναμνησθεὶς ὁ Πέτρος λέγει αὐτῷ·
Ῥαββί, ἴδε ἡ συκῆ ἣν κατηράσω ἐξήρανται.

22 καὶ ἀποκριθεὶς ὁ Ἰησοῦς λέγει αὐτοῖς·
Ἔχετε πίστιν θεοῦ· 23 ἀμὴν λέγω ὑμῖν ὅτι ὃς ἂν εἴπῃ τῷ ὄρει τούτῳ· Ἄρθητι καὶ βλήθητι εἰς τὴν θάλασσαν, καὶ μὴ διακριθῇ ἐν τῇ καρδίᾳ αὐτοῦ ἀλλὰ πιστεύῃ ὅτι ὃ λαλεῖ γίνεται, ἔσται αὐτῷ.
24 διὰ τοῦτο λέγω ὑμῖν, πάντα ὅσα προσεύχεσθε καὶ αἰτεῖσθε, πιστεύετε ὅτι ἐλάβετε, καὶ ἔσται ὑμῖν. 25 καὶ ὅταν στήκετε προσευχόμενοι, ἀφίετε εἴ τι ἔχετε κατά τινος, ἵνα καὶ ὁ πατὴρ ὑμῶν ὁ ἐν τοῖς οὐρανοῖς ἀφῇ ὑμῖν τὰ παραπτώματα ὑμῶν.

26 [Εἰ δὲ ὑμεῖς οὐκ ἀφίετε, οὐδὲ ὁ πατὴρ ὑμῶν ὁ ἐν τοῖς οὐρανοῖς ἀφήσει τὰ παραπτώματα ὑμῶν.]
27 Καὶ ἔρχονται πάλιν εἰς Ἱεροσόλυμα. καὶ ἐν τῷ ἱερῷ περιπατοῦντος αὐτοῦ ἔρχονται πρὸς αὐτὸν οἱ ἀρχιερεῖς καὶ οἱ γραμματεῖς καὶ οἱ πρεσβύτεροι

18 And the chief priests and the scribes heard, and they were seeking for how they would destroy him; for they were fearing him, for all the crowd was marveling at his
teaching. 19 And whenever evening came, he was exiting outside of the city. 20 And while passing by in the morning, they saw the fig tree having withered away from the
roots. 21 And after remembering, Peter begins saying to him, "Rabbi, look, the fig tree which you cursed has withered away." 22 And answering back, Jesus says to them,
"Have faith in God! 23 Amen! I am saying to you that whoever says to this mountain, 'Be lifted up and tossed into the sea,' and does not doubt in his heart but believes
that what he speaks happens, it will be to him. 24 On account of this I say to you *all*, everything, as much as you pray and ask for, believe that you received, and it will be
to you. 25 And whenever you *all* stand praying, forgive, if you have something against someone, in order that also your Father who is in heaven would forgive you your
trespasses. 26 *But if you yourselves do not forgive, neither will your Father who is in heaven forgive your trespasses.*" 27 And they come again into Jerusalem. And in the
temple, as he is walking around, the chief priests and the scribes and the elders come to him

28 καὶ ἔλεγον αὐτῷ·
Ἐν ποίᾳ ἐξουσίᾳ ταῦτα ποιεῖς; ἢ τίς σοι ἔδωκεν τὴν ἐξουσίαν ταύτην ἵνα ταῦτα ποιῇς;
29 ὁ δὲ Ἰησοῦς εἶπεν αὐτοῖς·
Ἐπερωτήσω ὑμᾶς ἕνα λόγον, καὶ ἀποκρίθητέ μοι, καὶ ἐρῶ ὑμῖν ἐν ποίᾳ ἐξουσίᾳ ταῦτα ποιῶ· 30 τὸ βάπτισμα τὸ Ἰωάννου ἐξ οὐρανοῦ ἦν ἢ ἐξ ἀνθρώπων; ἀποκρίθητέ μοι.

31 καὶ διελογίζοντο πρὸς ἑαυτοὺς λέγοντες·
Τί εἴπωμεν; ἐὰν εἴπωμεν· Ἐξ οὐρανοῦ, ἐρεῖ· Διὰ τί οὖν οὐκ ἐπιστεύσατε αὐτῷ;
32 ἀλλὰ εἴπωμεν· Ἐξ ἀνθρώπων,
—ἐφοβοῦντο τὸν ὄχλον, ἅπαντες γὰρ εἶχον τὸν Ἰωάννην ὄντως ὅτι προφήτης ἦν.

33 καὶ ἀποκριθέντες τῷ Ἰησοῦ λέγουσιν·
Οὐκ οἴδαμεν.

καὶ ὁ Ἰησοῦς λέγει αὐτοῖς·
Οὐδὲ ἐγὼ λέγω ὑμῖν ἐν ποίᾳ ἐξουσίᾳ ταῦτα ποιῶ.

Κεφ.
ΙΓ´

1 Καὶ ἤρξατο αὐτοῖς ἐν παραβολαῖς λαλεῖν·
Ἀμπελῶνα ἄνθρωπος ἐφύτευσεν,

καὶ περιέθηκεν φραγμὸν καὶ ὤρυξεν ὑπολήνιον καὶ ᾠκοδόμησεν πύργον, καὶ ἐξέδετο αὐτὸν γεωργοῖς, καὶ ἀπεδήμησεν.

2 καὶ ἀπέστειλεν πρὸς τοὺς γεωργοὺς τῷ καιρῷ δοῦλον, ἵνα παρὰ τῶν γεωργῶν λάβῃ ἀπὸ τῶν καρπῶν τοῦ ἀμπελῶνος·

28 and they kept saying to him, “By what authority are you doing these things? Or who gave you this authority in order that you would do these things?” 29 Well, Jesus said
to them, “I will ask you one thing, and answer back to me, and I will tell you by what authority I am doing these things. 30 The baptism of John, was it from heaven or from
heaven? Answer back to me.” 31 And they were reasoning among themselves saying, “What should we say? If we say, ‘From heaven,’ he will say, ‘Therefore, why did
you not believe him?’ 32 But should we say, ‘From people’?” They were fearing the crowd, for all people were holding that John really was a prophet. 33 And answering
back to Jesus, they say, “We don’t know.” And Jesus says to them, “Neither am I myself telling you by what authority I am doing these things.” 12:1 And he began to
speak to them in parables: “A person planted a vineyard, and he put a fence around it and he dug a pit for the winepress and he built a tower, and rented it out to farmers,
and he traveled afar. 2 And he sent to the farmers at the right time a servant, in order that from the farmers he would receive out of the fruits of the vineyard.

3 καὶ λαβόντες αὐτὸν ἔδειραν καὶ ἀπέστειλαν κενόν.

4 καὶ πάλιν ἀπέστειλεν πρὸς αὐτοὺς ἄλλον δοῦλον· κἀκεῖνον ἐκεφαλίωσαν καὶ ἠτίμασαν.
5 καὶ ἄλλον ἀπέστειλεν·

κἀκεῖνον ἀπέκτειναν, καὶ πολ-

λοὺς ἄλλους, οὓς μὲν δέροντες οὓς δὲ ἀποκτέννοντες.
6 ἔτι ἕνα εἶχεν, υἱὸν ἀγαπητόν· ἀπέστειλεν αὐτὸν ἔσχατον πρὸς αὐτοὺς λέγων ὅτι

Ἐντραπήσονται τὸν υἱόν μου.

7 ἐκεῖνοι δὲ οἱ γεωργοὶ πρὸς ἑαυτοὺς εἶπαν ὅτι

Οὗτός ἐστιν ὁ κληρονόμος· δεῦτε ἀποκτείνωμεν αὐτόν, καὶ ἡμῶν ἔσται ἡ κληρονομία.

8 καὶ λαβόντες ἀπέκτειναν αὐτόν, καὶ ἐξέβαλον αὐτὸν ἔξω τοῦ ἀμπελῶνος.

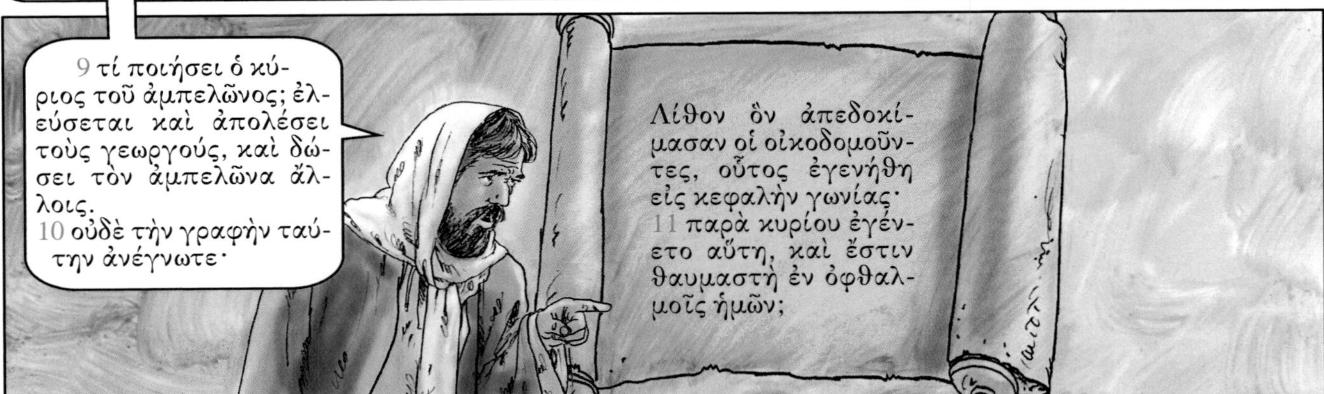
9 τί ποιήσει ὁ κύριος τοῦ ἀμπελῶνος; ἐλεύσεται καὶ ἀπολέσει τοὺς γεωργούς, καὶ δώσει τὸν ἀμπελῶνα ἄλλοις.
10 οὐδὲ τὴν γραφὴν ταύτην ἀνέγνωτε·
Λίθον ὃν ἀπεδοκίμασαν οἱ οἰκοδομοῦντες, οὗτος ἐγενήθη εἰς κεφαλὴν γωνίας·
11 παρὰ κυρίου ἐγένετο αὕτη, καὶ ἔστιν θαυμαστὴ ἐν ὀφθαλμοῖς ἡμῶν;

Διδάσκαλε, οἴδαμεν ὅτι ἀληθὴς εἶ καὶ οὐ μέλει σοι περὶ οὐδενός, οὐ γὰρ βλέπεις εἰς πρόσωπον ἀνθρώπων, ἀλλ᾽ ἐπ᾽ ἀληθείας τὴν ὁδὸν τοῦ θεοῦ διδάσκεις· ἔξεστιν δοῦναι κῆνσον Καίσαρι ἢ οὔ; δῶμεν ἢ μὴ δῶμεν;

Τί με πειράζετε; φέρετέ μοι δηνάριον ἵνα ἴδω.

16 οἱ δὲ ἤνεγκαν. καὶ λέγει αὐτοῖς·

Τίνος ἡ εἰκὼν αὕτη καὶ ἡ ἐπιγραφή;

3 And, after taking him, they beat him and sent him away empty. 4 And again he sent to them another servant; and that one they struck on the head and disrespected. 5 And
he sent another; and that one they killed, and *he sent* many others, some indeed *they were* beating, but some *they were* killing. 6 He still had one, a beloved son; he sent
him last to them saying this: 'They will respect my son.' 7 But those very farmers said to themselves this: 'This one is the heir; come, let us kill him, and ours will be the
inheritance!' 8 And, after taking him, they killed him, and cast him out, outside of the vineyard. 9 What will the master of the vineyard do? He will come and he will
remove the farmers, and he will give the vineyard to others. 10 Moreover, haven't you read this scripture: 'The stone, which the ones building rejected, this was made into
the head of the corner; 11 this happened from the Lord, and it is a marvel in our eyes?'" *Surely, yes!* 12 And they were seeking to seize him, and they feared the crowd, for
they understood that against them he had spoken the parable. And after leaving him, they departed. 13 And they begin sending to him some of the Pharisees and of the
Herodians, in order that they would trap him in word. 14 And after coming, they begin saying to him, "Teacher, we know that you are truthful and there is no concern for
you about anything, for you do not look at the reputation of people, but by truth you are teaching the way of God; is to pay tax to Caesar allowed, or not? Should we give
or should we not give?" 15 Well, he, knowing their hypocrisy, said to them, "Why are you testing me? Bring to me a denarius, in order that I would see *it*." 16 So, they
brought *it*. And he says to them, "Whose *is* this image? And the inscription?"

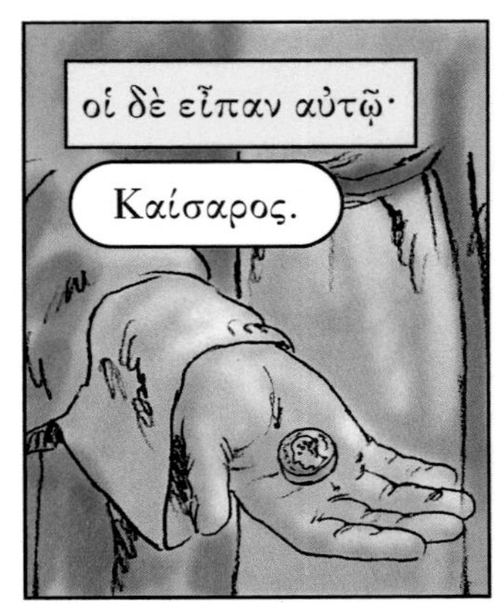
οἱ δὲ εἶπαν αὐτῷ·
Καίσαρος.

17 ὁ δὲ Ἰησοῦς εἶπεν αὐτοῖς·
Τὰ Καίσαρος ἀπόδοτε Καίσαρι καὶ τὰ τοῦ θεοῦ τῷ θεῷ.
καὶ ἐξεθαύμαζον ἐπ᾽ αὐτῷ.
18 Καὶ ἔρχονται Σαδδουκαῖοι πρὸς αὐτόν, οἵτινες λέγουσιν ἀνάστασιν μὴ εἶναι,

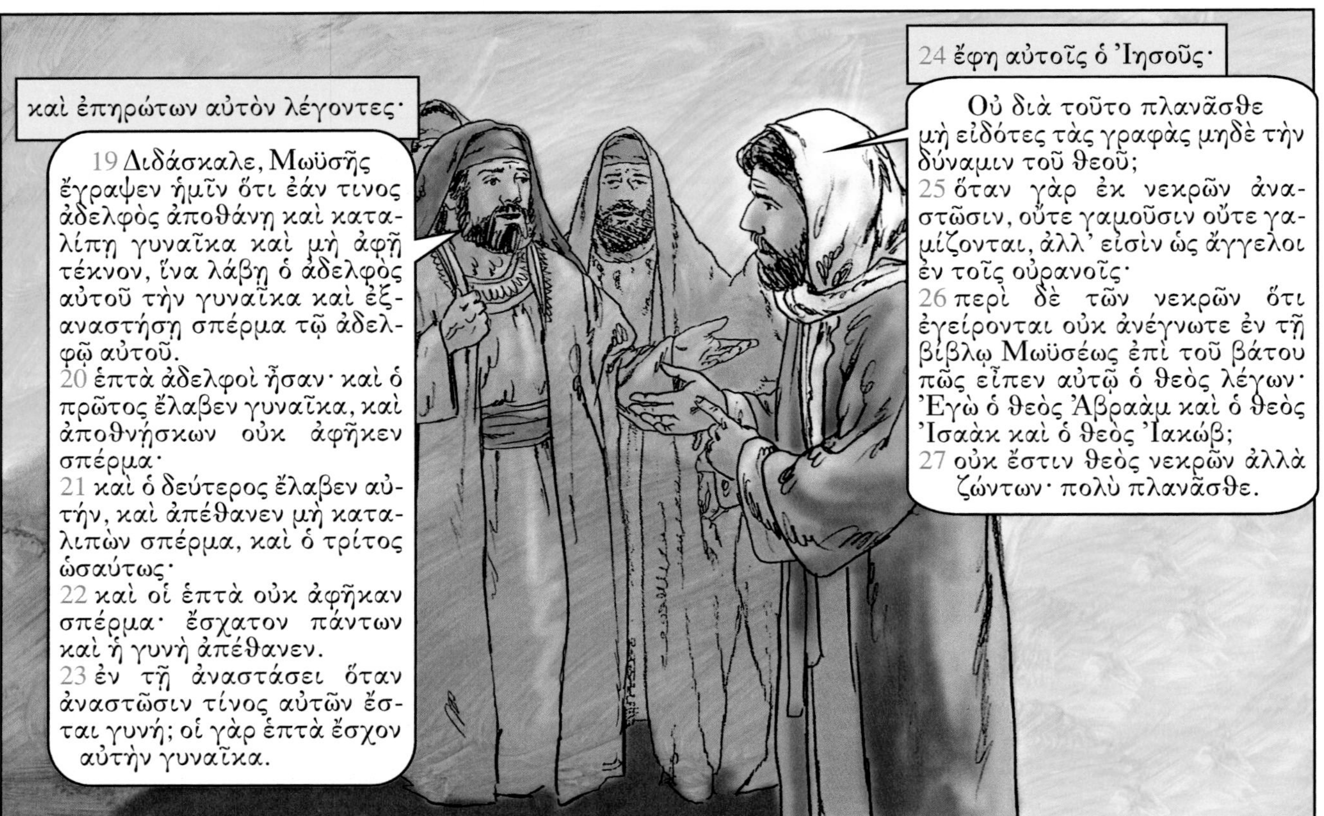
καὶ ἐπηρώτων αὐτὸν λέγοντες·
19 Διδάσκαλε, Μωϋσῆς ἔγραψεν ἡμῖν ὅτι ἐάν τινος ἀδελφὸς ἀποθάνῃ καὶ καταλίπῃ γυναῖκα καὶ μὴ ἀφῇ τέκνον, ἵνα λάβῃ ὁ ἀδελφὸς αὐτοῦ τὴν γυναῖκα καὶ ἐξαναστήσῃ σπέρμα τῷ ἀδελφῷ αὐτοῦ.
20 ἑπτὰ ἀδελφοὶ ἦσαν· καὶ ὁ πρῶτος ἔλαβεν γυναῖκα, καὶ ἀποθνήσκων οὐκ ἀφῆκεν σπέρμα·
21 καὶ ὁ δεύτερος ἔλαβεν αὐτήν, καὶ ἀπέθανεν μὴ καταλιπὼν σπέρμα, καὶ ὁ τρίτος ὡσαύτως·
22 καὶ οἱ ἑπτὰ οὐκ ἀφῆκαν σπέρμα· ἔσχατον πάντων καὶ ἡ γυνὴ ἀπέθανεν.
23 ἐν τῇ ἀναστάσει ὅταν ἀναστῶσιν τίνος αὐτῶν ἔσται γυνή; οἱ γὰρ ἑπτὰ ἔσχον αὐτὴν γυναῖκα.
24 ἔφη αὐτοῖς ὁ Ἰησοῦς·
Οὐ διὰ τοῦτο πλανᾶσθε μὴ εἰδότες τὰς γραφὰς μηδὲ τὴν δύναμιν τοῦ θεοῦ;
25 ὅταν γὰρ ἐκ νεκρῶν ἀναστῶσιν, οὔτε γαμοῦσιν οὔτε γαμίζονται, ἀλλ᾽ εἰσὶν ὡς ἄγγελοι ἐν τοῖς οὐρανοῖς·
26 περὶ δὲ τῶν νεκρῶν ὅτι ἐγείρονται οὐκ ἀνέγνωτε ἐν τῇ βίβλῳ Μωϋσέως ἐπὶ τοῦ βάτου πῶς εἶπεν αὐτῷ ὁ θεὸς λέγων· Ἐγὼ ὁ θεὸς Ἀβραὰμ καὶ ὁ θεὸς Ἰσαὰκ καὶ ὁ θεὸς Ἰακώβ;
27 οὐκ ἔστιν θεὸς νεκρῶν ἀλλὰ ζώντων· πολὺ πλανᾶσθε.

28 Καὶ προσελθὼν εἷς τῶν γραμματέων ἀκούσας αὐτῶν συζητούντων, ἰδὼν ὅτι καλῶς ἀπεκρίθη αὐτοῖς, ἐπηρώτησεν αὐτόν·

Ποία ἐστὶν ἐντολὴ πρώτη πάντων;

29 ἀπεκρίθη ὁ Ἰησοῦς ὅτι

Πρώτη ἐστίν· Ἄκουε, Ἰσραήλ, κύριος ὁ θεὸς ἡμῶν κύριος εἷς ἐστιν,
30 καὶ ἀγαπήσεις κύριον τὸν θεόν σου
ἐξ ὅλης τῆς καρδίας σου καὶ ἐξ ὅλης τῆς ψυχῆς σου καὶ ἐξ ὅλης τῆς διανοίας σου καὶ ἐξ ὅλης τῆς ἰσχύος σου.

So, they said to him, "Caesar's." 17 Well, Jesus said to them, "The things of Caesar give to Caesar and the things of God to God!" And they were marveling greatly at him.
18 And the Sadducees come to him, who say that there is no resurrection, and they were asking him saying, 19 "Teacher, Moses wrote to us that if a brother of some man
dies and he leaves behind a wife and leaves no child, that his brother would take his wife and raise up offspring for his brother. 20 There were seven brothers; and the first
took a wife, and, when dying, he left no offspring; 21 and the second took her, and he died not leaving behind offspring, and the third likewise; 22 and the seven left no offspring; last of all also the wife died. 23 In the resurrection, whenever they arise, which of theirs will the wife be? For the seven had her as a wife." 24 Jesus continued saying
to them, "Aren't you deceived about this, not knowing the Scriptures, nor the power of God? *Surely, yes!* 25 For whenever they arise from the dead, neither do they marry
nor are they given in marriage, but they are like angels in the heavens. 26 Moreover, concerning the dead, that they are raised up, haven't you read in the Book of Moses
about the bush, how God spoke to him saying, 'I am the God of Abraham and the God of Isaac and the God of Jacob?' *Surely, yes!* 27 He is not the God of the dead but of
the living! You are much deceived!" 28 And after coming, one of the scribes hearing them disputing, knowing that he had answered back to them well, asked him, "Which
kind of commandment is first of all? 29 Jesus answered back indeed, "The first is, 'Hear, O Israel, the Lord our God, the Lord is one'; 30 and 'You shall love the Lord your
God from your whole heart, and from your whole soul, and from your whole mind, and from your whole strength.'

ευτ ρα α τη·
Ἀγαπήσεις τὸν πλησίον σου ὡς σεαυτόν. μείζων τούτων ἄλλη ἐντολὴ οὐκ ἔστιν.
Καλῶς, διδάσκαλε, ἐπ' ἀληθείας εἶπες ὅτι εἷς ἐστιν καὶ οὐκ ἔστιν ἄλλος πλὴν αὐτοῦ·
33 καὶ τὸ ἀγαπᾶν αὐτὸν ἐξ ὅλης τῆς καρδίας καὶ ἐξ ὅλης τῆς συνέσεως καὶ ἐξ ὅλης τῆς ἰσχύος καὶ τὸ ἀγαπᾶν τὸν πλησίον ὡς ἑαυτὸν περισσότερόν ἐστιν πάντων τῶν ὁλοκαυτωμάτων καὶ θυσιῶν.

34 καὶ ὁ Ἰησοῦς ἰδὼν αὐτὸν ὅτι νουνεχῶς ἀπεκρίθη εἶπεν αὐτῷ·
Οὐ μακρὰν εἶ ἀπὸ τῆς βασιλείας τοῦ θεοῦ.
καὶ οὐδεὶς οὐκέτι ἐτόλμα αὐτὸν ἐπερωτῆσαι.
35 Καὶ ἀποκριθεὶς ὁ Ἰησοῦς ἔλεγεν διδάσκων ἐν τῷ ἱερῷ·
Πῶς λέγουσιν οἱ γραμματεῖς ὅτι ὁ χριστὸς υἱὸς Δαυίδ ἐστιν;

36 αὐτὸς Δαυὶδ εἶπεν ἐν τῷ πνεύματι τῷ ἁγίῳ·
Εἶπεν κύριος τῷ κυρίῳ μου· Κάθου ἐκ δεξιῶν μου ἕως ἂν θῶ τοὺς ἐχθρούς σου ὑποκάτω τῶν ποδῶν σου.
37 αὐτὸς Δαυὶδ λέγει αὐτὸν κύριον, καὶ πόθεν αὐτοῦ ἐστιν υἱός;

καὶ ὁ πολὺς ὄχλος ἤκουεν αὐτοῦ ἡδέως.

38 Καὶ ἐν τῇ διδαχῇ αὐτοῦ ἔλεγεν·
Βλέπετε ἀπὸ τῶν γραμματέων τῶν θελόντων ἐν στολαῖς περιπατεῖν καὶ ἀσπασμοὺς ἐν ταῖς ἀγοραῖς
39 καὶ πρωτοκαθεδρίας ἐν ταῖς συναγωγαῖς καὶ πρωτοκλισίας ἐν τοῖς δείπνοις,
40 οἱ κατεσθίοντες τὰς οἰκίας τῶν χηρῶν καὶ προφάσει μακρὰ προσευχόμενοι· οὗτοι λήμψονται περισσότερον κρίμα.

31 The second is this, 'You shall love your neighbor as yourself.' There is no other commandment greater than these!" 32 And the scribe said to him, "Excellent, Teacher,
in truth you said that 'He is one' and 'There is no other except him'; 33 and 'To love him from the whole heart, and from the whole understanding, and from the whole
strength,' and 'To love the neighbor as oneself, is much more than all burnt-offerings and sacrifices.'" 34 And Jesus, after seeing him, that he had wisely answered back,
said to him, "Not far are you from the Kingdom of God." And no one any longer was daring to question him. 35 And answering back, Jesus was saying, teaching in the
temple, "How do the scribes keep saying that the Christ is the Son of David? 36 David himself said by the Holy Spirit, 'The Lord said to my Lord, 'Sit at my right until I
place your enemies under your feet.'' 37 David himself is saying *that* he *is* Lord, and where is his son from?" And the large crowd was listening to him happily. 38 And in
his teaching he was saying, "Beware of the scribes who want in long robes to walk and *want* greetings in the marketplaces 39 and chief seats in the synagogues and chief
places at the feasts, 40 the ones devouring the houses of the widows and in pretense praying long prayers; they shall receive greater condemnation."

41 Καὶ καθίσας κατέναντι τοῦ γαζοφυλακίου ἐθεώρει πῶς ὁ ὄχλος βάλλει χαλκὸν εἰς τὸ γαζοφυλάκιον· καὶ πολλοὶ πλούσιοι ἔβαλλον πολλά·
42 καὶ ἐλθοῦσα μία χήρα πτωχὴ ἔβαλεν λεπτὰ δύο, ὅ ἐστιν κοδράντης.

43 καὶ προσκαλεσάμενος τοὺς μαθητὰς αὐτοῦ εἶπεν αὐτοῖς·
Ἀμὴν λέγω ὑμῖν ὅτι ἡ χήρα αὕτη ἡ πτωχὴ πλεῖον πάντων ἔβαλεν τῶν βαλλόντων εἰς τὸ γαζοφυλάκιον· 44 πάντες γὰρ ἐκ τοῦ περισσεύοντος αὐτοῖς ἔβαλον, αὕτη δὲ ἐκ τῆς ὑστερήσεως αὐτῆς πάντα ὅσα εἶχεν ἔβαλεν, ὅλον τὸν βίον αὐτῆς.

Κεφ. ΙΔ´

1 Καὶ ἐκπορευομένου αὐτοῦ ἐκ τοῦ ἱεροῦ λέγει αὐτῷ εἷς τῶν μαθητῶν αὐτοῦ·
Διδάσκαλε, ἴδε ποταποὶ λίθοι καὶ ποταπαὶ οἰκοδομαί.

2 καὶ ὁ Ἰησοῦς εἶπεν αὐτῷ·
Βλέπεις ταύτας τὰς μεγάλας οἰκοδομάς; οὐ μὴ ἀφεθῇ ὧδε λίθος ἐπὶ λίθον ὃς οὐ μὴ καταλυθῇ.

3 Καὶ καθημένου αὐτοῦ εἰς τὸ Ὄρος τῶν Ἐλαιῶν κατέναντι τοῦ ἱεροῦ ἐπηρώτα αὐτὸν κατ’ ἰδίαν Πέτρος καὶ Ἰάκωβος καὶ Ἰωάννης καὶ Ἀνδρέας·
4 Εἰπὸν ἡμῖν πότε ταῦτα ἔσται, καὶ τί τὸ σημεῖον ὅταν μέλλῃ ταῦτα συντελεῖσθαι πάντα.

[41] And after sitting down in front of the treasury, he was watching how the crowd was casting coins into the treasury; and many rich people were casting in many. [42] And
after coming, one poor widow cast in two lepta, which is a quadrans. [43] And after calling to his disciples, he said to them, "Amen! I am saying to you that this poor widow
cast in more than all the ones who are casting into the treasury; [44] for they all cast in from their abundance, but this woman from her poverty cast in all, how much she was
having, her whole means of living!" 13:1 And while he was walking out of the temple, one of his disciples begins saying to him, "Teacher, look what quality the stones
are and what quality the buildings are!" [2] And Jesus said to him, "Are you seeing these great buildings? Not ever here will a stone be left upon a stone, which will not
surely be destroyed!" [3] And while he was sitting in the Mount of Olives opposite of the temple, Peter was asking him in private, and James and John and Andrew, [4] "Tell
us, when will these things be, and what is the sign whenever all these things are about to be accomplished?"

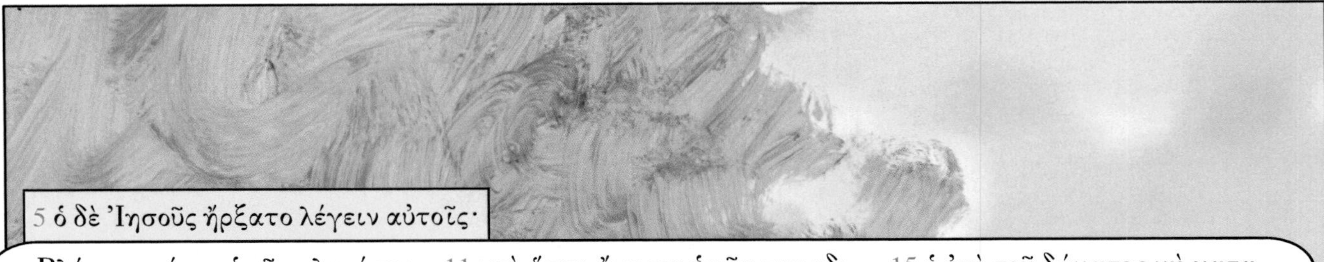
5 ὁ δὲ Ἰησοῦς ἤρξατο λέγειν αὐτοῖς·

Βλέπετε μή τις ὑμᾶς πλανήσῃ·
6 πολλοὶ ἐλεύσονται ἐπὶ τῷ ὀνόματί μου λέγοντες ὅτι Ἐγώ εἰμι,
καὶ πολλοὺς πλανήσουσιν.
7 ὅταν δὲ ἀκούσητε πολέμους καὶ
ἀκοὰς πολέμων, μὴ θροεῖσθε· δεῖ
γενέσθαι, ἀλλ᾽ οὔπω τὸ τέλος.
8 ἐγερθήσεται γὰρ ἔθνος ἐπ᾽ ἔθνος καὶ βασιλεία ἐπὶ βασιλείαν,
ἔσονται σεισμοὶ κατὰ τόπους,
⸀ἔσονται λιμοί· ἀρχὴ ὠδίνων ταῦτα.
9 βλέπετε δὲ ὑμεῖς ἑαυτούς· παραδώσουσιν ὑμᾶς εἰς συνέδρια καὶ
εἰς συναγωγὰς δαρήσεσθε καὶ ἐπὶ
ἡγεμόνων καὶ βασιλέων σταθήσε-
σθε ἕνεκεν ἐμοῦ εἰς μαρτύριον
αὐτοῖς.
10 καὶ εἰς πάντα τὰ ἔθνη πρῶτον
δεῖ κηρυχθῆναι τὸ εὐαγγέλιον.
11 καὶ ὅταν ἄγωσιν ὑμᾶς παραδι-
δόντες, μὴ προμεριμνᾶτε τί λαλή-
σητε, ἀλλ᾽ ὃ ἐὰν δοθῇ ὑμῖν ἐν
ἐκείνῃ τῇ ὥρᾳ τοῦτο λαλεῖτε, οὐ
γάρ ἐστε ὑμεῖς οἱ λαλοῦντες ἀλλὰ
τὸ πνεῦμα τὸ ἅγιον.
12 καὶ παραδώσει ἀδελφὸς ἀδελφὸν εἰς θάνατον καὶ πατὴρ τέκνον, καὶ ἐπαναστήσονται τέκνα
ἐπὶ γονεῖς καὶ θανατώσουσιν αὐ-
τούς·
13 καὶ ἔσεσθε μισούμενοι ὑπὸ
πάντων διὰ τὸ ὄνομά μου. ὁ δὲ
ὑπομείνας εἰς τέλος οὗτος σωθήσεται.
14 Ὅταν δὲ ἴδητε τὸ βδέλυγμα
τῆς ἐρημώσεως ἑστηκότα ὅπου οὐ
δεῖ, ὁ ἀναγινώσκων νοείτω, τότε
οἱ ἐν τῇ Ἰουδαίᾳ φευγέτωσαν εἰς
τὰ ὄρη,
15 ὁ ἐπὶ τοῦ δώματος μὴ καταβάτω μηδὲ εἰσελθάτω τι ἆραι ἐκ
τῆς οἰκίας αὐτοῦ,
16 καὶ ὁ εἰς τὸν ἀγρὸν μὴ ἐπι-
στρεψάτω εἰς τὰ ὀπίσω ἆραι τὸ
ἱμάτιον αὐτοῦ.
17 οὐαὶ δὲ ταῖς ἐν γαστρὶ ἐχούσαις
καὶ ταῖς θηλαζούσαις ἐν ἐκείναις
ταῖς ἡμέραις.
18 προσεύχεσθε δὲ ἵνα μὴ γένηται
χειμῶνος·
19 ἔσονται γὰρ αἱ ἡμέραι ἐκεῖναι
θλῖψις οἵα οὐ γέγονεν τοιαύτη
ἀπ᾽ ἀρχῆς κτίσεως ἣν ἔκτισεν ὁ
θεὸς ἕως τοῦ νῦν καὶ οὐ μὴ γένηται.
20 καὶ εἰ μὴ ἐκολόβωσεν κύριος
τὰς ἡμέρας, οὐκ ἂν ἐσώθη πᾶσα
σάρξ. ἀλλὰ διὰ τοὺς ἐκλεκτοὺς
οὓς ἐξελέξατο ἐκολόβωσεν τὰς
ἡμέρας.

[5] Well, Jesus began to say to them, "Beware lest someone leads you astray! [6] Many will come in my name saying this: 'I am,' and many they will lead astray. [7] Moreover,
whenever you hear of wars and rumors of wars, do not be troubled! It must happen, but it is not yet the end. [8] For nation will rise against nation and kingdom against
kingdom, there will be earthquakes in many places, there will be famines; these things are the beginnings of agony. [9] So, you yourselves be aware *concerning* yourselves!
They will hand you over to councils and at synagogues you will be flogged and before rulers and kings you will stand on account of me as a witness to them. [10] And into
all the nations first the gospel must be proclaimed. [11] And whenever they lead you handing *you* over, do not be anxious beforehand what you will say, but, whatever is
given to you in that very hour, speak this, for you yourselves are not the ones speaking but the Holy Spirit. [12] And a brother will hand over a brother unto death and a father
a child, and children will rise up against parents and they will put them to death. [13] And you will continue being hated by all people because of my name. But the one
enduring to the end, this one will be saved. [14] Moreover, whenever you see the abomination of desolation standing where it must not (let the one reading understand!), at
that time let the ones in Judaea flee into the mountains [15] and let not the one on the roof go down nor enter to take something from his house, [16] and let not the one in the
field return for the things behind to take his clothing. [17] Moreover, woe to those having *a child* in the womb and to the ones nursing in those days! [18] So, pray that it would
not happen during winter! [19] For those days will be a hardship, of such a kind that this sort of thing has not occurred from the beginning of creation, which God created,
until the present and will never ever occur. [20] And if the Lord had not shortened the days, every physical person would not have been saved. But on account of the chosen
ones, whom he chose, he shortened the days.

21 καὶ τότε ἐάν τις ὑμῖν εἴπῃ· Ἴδε ὧδε ὁ χριστός, Ἴδε ἐκεῖ, μὴ πιστεύετε·

22 ἐγερθήσονται γὰρ ψευδόχριστοι καὶ ψευδοπροφῆται καὶ δώσουσιν σημεῖα καὶ τέρατα πρὸς τὸ ἀποπλανᾶν εἰ δυνατὸν τοὺς ἐκλεκτούς·

23 ὑμεῖς δὲ βλέπετε· προείρηκα ὑμῖν πάντα.

24 Ἀλλὰ ἐν ἐκείναις ταῖς ἡμέραις μετὰ τὴν θλῖψιν ἐκείνην

ὁ ἥλιος σκοτισθήσεται, καὶ ἡ σελήνη οὐ δώσει τὸ φέγγος αὐτῆς,

25 καὶ οἱ ἀστέρες ἔσονται ἐκ τοῦ οὐρανοῦ πίπτοντες, καὶ αἱ δυνάμεις αἱ ἐν τοῖς οὐρανοῖς σαλευθήσονται.

26 καὶ τότε ὄψονται τὸν υἱὸν τοῦ ἀνθρώπου ἐρχόμενον ἐν νεφέλαις μετὰ δυνάμεως πολλῆς καὶ δόξης·

27 καὶ τότε ἀποστελεῖ τοὺς ἀγγέλους καὶ ἐπισυνάξει τοὺς ἐκλεκτοὺς ἐκ τῶν τεσσάρων ἀνέμων ἀπ' ἄκρου γῆς ἕως ἄκρου οὐρανοῦ.

28 Ἀπὸ δὲ τῆς συκῆς μάθετε τὴν παραβολήν· ὅταν ἤδη ὁ κλάδος αὐτῆς ἁπαλὸς γένηται καὶ ἐκφύῃ τὰ φύλλα, γινώσκετε ὅτι ἐγγὺς τὸ θέρος ἐστίν·

29 οὕτως καὶ ὑμεῖς, ὅταν ἴδητε ταῦτα γινόμενα, γινώσκετε ὅτι ἐγγύς ἐστιν ἐπὶ θύραις.

30 ἀμὴν λέγω ὑμῖν ὅτι οὐ μὴ παρέλθῃ ἡ γενεὰ αὕτη μέχρις οὗ ταῦτα πάντα γένηται.

31 ὁ οὐρανὸς καὶ ἡ γῆ παρελεύσονται, οἱ δὲ λόγοι μου οὐ μὴ ⸀παρελεύσονται.

32 Περὶ δὲ τῆς ἡμέρας ἐκείνης ἢ τῆς ὥρας οὐδεὶς οἶδεν, οὐδὲ οἱ ἄγγελοι ἐν οὐρανῷ οὐδὲ ὁ υἱός, εἰ μὴ ὁ πατήρ.

33 βλέπετε ἀγρυπνεῖτε, οὐκ οἴδατε γὰρ πότε ὁ καιρός ἐστιν·

34 ὡς ἄνθρωπος ἀπόδημος ἀφεὶς τὴν οἰκίαν αὐτοῦ καὶ δοὺς τοῖς δούλοις αὐτοῦ τὴν ἐξουσίαν, ἑκάστῳ τὸ ἔργον αὐτοῦ, καὶ τῷ θυρωρῷ ἐνετείλατο ἵνα γρηγορῇ.

35 γρηγορεῖτε οὖν, οὐκ οἴδατε γὰρ πότε ὁ κύριος τῆς οἰκίας ἔρχεται, ἢ ὀψὲ ἢ μεσονύκτιον ἢ ἀλεκτοροφωνίας ἢ πρωΐ,

36 μὴ ἐλθὼν ἐξαίφνης εὕρῃ ὑμᾶς καθεύδοντας·

37 ὃ δὲ ὑμῖν λέγω πᾶσιν λέγω· γρηγορεῖτε.

21 And at that time, if someone says to you *all*, 'Look, here is the Messiah,' 'Look, there,' do not be trusting *it*! 22 For false messiahs and false prophets will arise and they
will give signs and wonders in order to lead astray, if possible, the chosen ones. 23 But you yourselves be aware! I have told you about all things beforehand. 24 But in those
very days after that hardship, the sun will be darkened, and the moon will not give its light, 25 and the stars will be falling from heaven, and the powers in the heavens will
be shaken. 26 And at that time they will see the Son of Man coming in clouds with much power and glory. 27 And at that time he will send the messengers and he will gather
together the chosen ones from the four winds from the farthest part of the earth until the farthest part of heaven. 28 Moreover, from the fig tree learn the parable: whenever
its branch has already become tender and puts out the leaves, know that the summer is near; 29 thus also you yourselves, whenever you see these things occurring, you will
know that it is near at the doors. 30 Amen! I am saying to you that this generation will never ever pass away until all these things occur. 31 Heaven and earth will pass away,
but my words will never ever pass away. 32 But concerning that day or hour no one knows, neither the angels in heaven nor the Son, except the Father. 33 Be aware! Be
alert! For you do not know when the time is. 34 *It is* like a traveling person leaving his house and giving the authority to his servants, to each one his work, and he commanded
the gatekeeper in order that he would keep watch. 35 Therefore, keep watchful, for you do not know when the lord of the house comes, whether evening or midnight or
during the rooster's crowing or early in the morning, 36 lest, after coming suddenly, he finds you sleeping. 37 Well, that which I am saying to you, I say to all: Keep
watchful!"

Κεφ. ΙΕ´

1 Ἦν δὲ τὸ πάσχα καὶ τὰ ἄζυμα μετὰ δύο ἡμέρας. καὶ ἐζήτουν οἱ ἀρχιερεῖς καὶ οἱ γραμματεῖς πῶς αὐτὸν ἐν δόλῳ κρατήσαντες ἀποκτείνωσιν, 2 ἔλεγον γάρ·
Μὴ ἐν τῇ ἑορτῇ, μήποτε ἔσται θόρυβος τοῦ λαοῦ.

3 Καὶ ὄντος αὐτοῦ ἐν Βηθανίᾳ ἐν τῇ οἰκίᾳ Σίμωνος τοῦ λεπροῦ κατακειμένου αὐτοῦ ἦλθεν γυνὴ ἔχουσα ἀλάβαστρον μύρου νάρδου πιστικῆς πολυτελοῦς· συντρίψασα τὴν ἀλάβαστρον κατέχεεν αὐτοῦ τῆς κεφαλῆς.

4 ἦσαν δέ τινες ἀγανακτοῦντες πρὸς ἑαυτούς·
Εἰς τί ἡ ἀπώλεια αὕτη τοῦ μύρου γέγονεν; 5 ἠδύνατο γὰρ τοῦτο τὸ μύρον πραθῆναι ἐπάνω δηναρίων τριακοσίων καὶ δοθῆναι τοῖς πτωχοῖς·
καὶ ἐνεβριμῶντο αὐτῇ.

6 ὁ δὲ Ἰησοῦς εἶπεν·
Ἄφετε αὐτήν· τί αὐτῇ κόπους παρέχετε; καλὸν ἔργον ἠργάσατο ἐν ἐμοί·

7 πάντοτε γὰρ τοὺς πτωχοὺς ἔχετε μεθ᾽ ἑαυτῶν, καὶ ὅταν θέλητε δύνασθε αὐτοῖς εὖ ποιῆσαι, ἐμὲ δὲ οὐ πάντοτε ἔχετε·

8 ὃ ἔσχεν ἐποίησεν, προέλαβεν μυρίσαι τὸ σῶμά μου εἰς τὸν ἐνταφιασμόν.

9 ἀμὴν δὲ λέγω ὑμῖν, ὅπου ἐὰν κηρυχθῇ τὸ εὐαγγέλιον εἰς ὅλον τὸν κόσμον, καὶ ὃ ἐποίησεν αὕτη λαληθήσεται εἰς μνημόσυνον αὐτῆς.

14:1 Well, it was the Passover and the Unleavened Bread in two days. And the chief priests and the scribes were seeking how, *by* catching him with deceit, they would
kill *him*, 2 for they kept saying, "Not during the feast, in order that there would not be an uproar by the people!" 3 And while he was in Bethany sitting in the house of
Simon the leper, a woman came having an alabaster jar of very costly myrrh of pure nard; after breaking the jar, she was pouring it over his head. 4 But some were becoming
indignant among themselves, "To what end has this waste of myrrh occurred? 5 For this myrrh was able to be sold for more than three hundred denarii and to be given to
the poor." And they were complaining to her. 6 Well, Jesus said, "Leave her alone; why are you *all* causing troubles for her? A good deed she did for me! 7 For always you
continue having the poor with yourselves, and whenever you want, you are able to do good for them, but me, you do not always have! 8 That which she had, she did; she
planned to anoint my body for burial. 9 Amen! Moreover, I am saying to you, wherever the gospel is preached in the whole world, also that which this woman did will be
spoken to remember her."

10 Καὶ Ἰούδας Ἰσκαριὼθ ὁ εἷς τῶν δώδεκα ἀπῆλθεν πρὸς τοὺς ἀρχιερεῖς ἵνα αὐτὸν παραδοῖ αὐτοῖς.
11 οἱ δὲ ἀκούσαντες ἐχάρησαν καὶ ἐπηγγείλαντο αὐτῷ ἀργύριον δοῦναι. καὶ ἐζήτει πῶς αὐτὸν εὐκαίρως παραδοῖ.

12 Καὶ τῇ πρώτῃ ἡμέρᾳ τῶν ἀζύμων, ὅτε τὸ πάσχα ἔθυον, λέγουσιν αὐτῷ οἱ μαθηταὶ αὐτοῦ·
Ποῦ θέλεις ἀπελθόντες ἑτοιμάσωμεν ἵνα φάγῃς τὸ πάσχα;
13 καὶ ἀποστέλλει δύο τῶν μαθητῶν αὐτοῦ καὶ λέγει αὐτοῖς·
Ὑπάγετε εἰς τὴν πόλιν, καὶ ἀπαντήσει ὑμῖν ἄνθρωπος κεράμιον ὕδατος βαστάζων· ἀκολουθήσατε αὐτῷ, 14 καὶ ὅπου ἐὰν εἰσέλθῃ εἴπατε τῷ οἰκοδεσπότῃ ὅτι Ὁ διδάσκαλος λέγει· Ποῦ ἐστιν τὸ κατάλυμά μου ὅπου τὸ πάσχα μετὰ τῶν μαθητῶν μου φάγω;

15 καὶ αὐτὸς ὑμῖν δείξει ἀνάγαιον μέγα ἐστρωμένον ἕτοιμον· καὶ ἐκεῖ ἑτοιμάσατε ἡμῖν.

16 καὶ ἐξῆλθον οἱ μαθηταὶ καὶ ἦλθον εἰς τὴν πόλιν καὶ εὗρον καθὼς εἶπεν αὐτοῖς, καὶ ἡτοίμασαν τὸ πάσχα.
17 Καὶ ὀψίας γενομένης ἔρχεται μετὰ τῶν δώδεκα.

18 καὶ ἀνακειμένων αὐτῶν καὶ ἐσθιόντων ὁ Ἰησοῦς εἶπεν·
Ἀμὴν λέγω ὑμῖν ὅτι εἷς ἐξ ὑμῶν παραδώσει με ὁ ἐσθίων μετ' ἐμοῦ.

10 And Judas Iscariot, one of the twelve, went away to the chief priests, in order that he would hand him over to them. 11 Well, they, after hearing, were glad and promised
to give to him money. And he was seeking how he would hand him over at an opportune time. 12 And on the first day of unleavened loaves, when they were sacrificing
the Passover, his disciples begin saying to him, "Where do you want that, after departing, we should prepare in order that you would eat the Passover?" 13 And he sends
two of his disciples and says to them, "Go into the city, and a person carrying a pitcher of water will meet you; follow him, 14 and, wherever he enters, say to the master
of the house this: "The Teacher says, 'Where is my upper-room where I will eat the Passover with my disciples?' 15 And he himself will show to you a large upper room
already furnished; and there prepare it for us." 16 And the disciples went out and came into the city and found *it* just as he said to them, and they prepared the Passover.
17 And after evening came, he comes with the Twelve. 18 And while they were reclining and eating, Jesus said, "Amen! I am saying to you that one of you will hand me
over, *namely,* the one eating with me."

ἤρξαντο λυπεῖσθαι καὶ λέγειν αὐτῷ εἷς κατὰ εἷς·
Μήτι ἐγώ;

20 ὁ δὲ εἶπεν αὐτοῖς·
Εἷς τῶν δώδεκα, ὁ ἐμβαπτόμενος μετ᾽ ἐμοῦ εἰς τὸ τρύβλιον·

21 ὅτι ὁ μὲν υἱὸς τοῦ ἀνθρώπου ὑπάγει καθὼς γέγραπται περὶ αὐτοῦ, οὐαὶ δὲ τῷ ἀνθρώπῳ ἐκείνῳ δι᾽ οὗ ὁ υἱὸς τοῦ ἀνθρώπου παραδίδοται· καλὸν αὐτῷ εἰ οὐκ ἐγεννήθη ὁ ἄνθρωπος ἐκεῖνος.

22 Καὶ ἐσθιόντων αὐτῶν λαβὼν ἄρτον εὐλογήσας ἔκλασεν καὶ ἔδωκεν αὐτοῖς

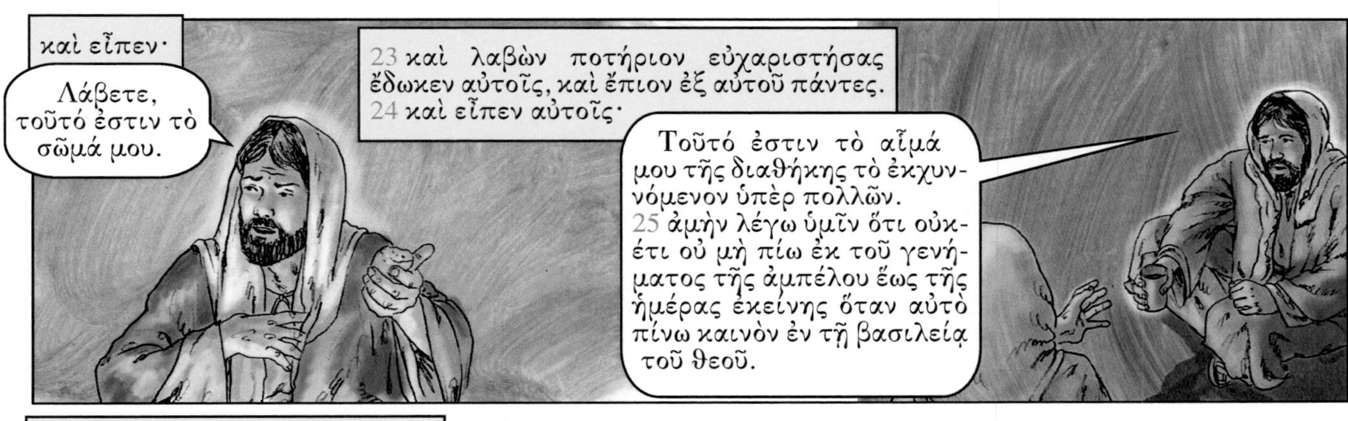

καὶ εἶπεν·
Λάβετε, τοῦτό ἐστιν τὸ σῶμά μου.
23 καὶ λαβὼν ποτήριον εὐχαριστήσας ἔδωκεν αὐτοῖς, καὶ ἔπιον ἐξ αὐτοῦ πάντες. 24 καὶ εἶπεν αὐτοῖς·
Τοῦτό ἐστιν τὸ αἷμά μου τῆς διαθήκης τὸ ἐκχυννόμενον ὑπὲρ πολλῶν. 25 ἀμὴν λέγω ὑμῖν ὅτι οὐκέτι οὐ μὴ πίω ἐκ τοῦ γενήματος τῆς ἀμπέλου ἕως τῆς ἡμέρας ἐκείνης ὅταν αὐτὸ πίνω καινὸν ἐν τῇ βασιλείᾳ τοῦ θεοῦ.

26 Καὶ ὑμνήσαντες ἐξῆλθον εἰς τὸ Ὄρος τῶν Ἐλαιῶν.
27 Καὶ λέγει αὐτοῖς ὁ Ἰησοῦς ὅτι
Πάντες σκανδαλισθήσεσθε, ὅτι γέγραπται·
Πατάξω τὸν ποιμένα, καὶ τὰ πρόβατα διασκορπισθήσονται.
28 ἀλλὰ μετὰ τὸ ἐγερθῆναί με προάξω ὑμᾶς εἰς τὴν Γαλιλαίαν.

29 ὁ δὲ Πέτρος ἔφη αὐτῷ·

Εἰ καὶ πάντες σκανδαλισθήσονται, ἀλλ᾽ οὐκ ἐγώ.

19 They began to be grieved and to say to him one-by-one, "Not I, is it? *Surely, no!*" 20 Well, he said to them, "One of the twelve, the one dipping with me into the bowl;
21 because, on the one hand, the Son of Man is departing just as it has been written about him, but on the other hand, woe to that person through whom the Son of Man is
handed over! It would good for him if that man had not been born. 22 And, while they were eating, taking bread, after giving blessing, he broke and gave *it* to them and
said, "Take, this is my body." 23 And taking a cup, after giving thanks, he gave *it* to them, and they all drank from it. 24 And he said to them, "This is my blood of the
covenant being poured out for many. 25 Amen! I am saying to you that no longer will I ever I drink from the fruit of the vine until that day whenever I drink it anew in the
Kingdom of God." 26 And after singing a hymn, they went out into the Mount of Olives. 27 And Jesus begins saying to them indeed, "All of you will stumble, because it
has been written, 'I will strike the shepherd, and the sheep will be scattered widely.' 28 But after I am raised up, I will go before you into Galilee." 29 So, Peter was saying
to him, "Even if all will stumble, however I will not!"

30 καὶ λέγει αὐτῷ ὁ Ἰησοῦς·
Ἀμὴν λέγω σοι ὅτι σὺ σήμερον ταύτῃ τῇ νυκτὶ πρὶν ἢ δὶς ἀλέκτορα φωνῆσαι τρίς με ἀπαρνήσῃ.
31 ὁ δὲ ἐκπερισσῶς ἐλάλει·
Ἐὰν δέῃ με συναποθανεῖν σοι, οὐ μή σε ἀπαρνήσομαι.
ὡσαύτως δὲ καὶ πάντες ἔλεγον.

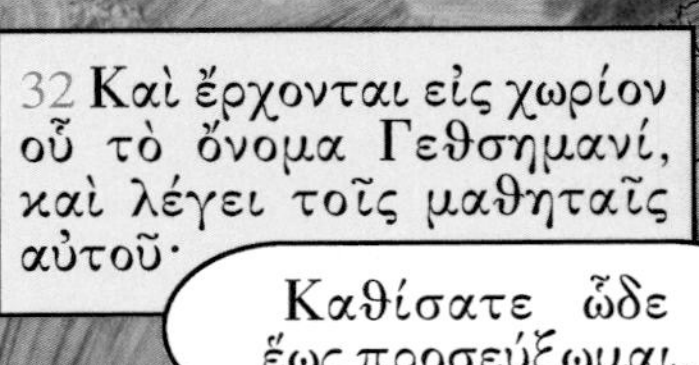

32 Καὶ ἔρχονται εἰς χωρίον οὗ τὸ ὄνομα Γεθσημανί, καὶ λέγει τοῖς μαθηταῖς αὐτοῦ·
Καθίσατε ὧδε ἕως προσεύξωμαι.
33 καὶ παραλαμβάνει τὸν Πέτρον καὶ Ἰάκωβον καὶ Ἰωάννην μετ᾽ αὐτοῦ, καὶ ἤρξατο ἐκθαμβεῖσθαι καὶ ἀδημονεῖν,

34 καὶ λέγει αὐτοῖς·
Περίλυπός ἐστιν ἡ ψυχή μου ἕως θανάτου·

μείνατε ὧδε καὶ γρηγορεῖτε.

35 καὶ προελθὼν μικρὸν ἔπιπτεν ἐπὶ τῆς γῆς, καὶ προσηύχετο ἵνα εἰ δυνατόν ἐστιν παρέλθῃ ἀπ᾽ αὐτοῦ ἡ ὥρα,

36 καὶ ἔλεγεν·
Αββα ὁ πατήρ, πάντα δυνατά σοι· παρένεγκε τὸ ποτήριον τοῦτο ἀπ᾽ ἐμοῦ·

ἀλλ᾽ οὐ τί ἐγὼ θέλω ἀλλὰ τί σύ.

37 καὶ ἔρχεται καὶ εὑρίσκει αὐτοὺς καθεύδοντας, καὶ λέγει τῷ Πέτρῳ·
Σίμων, καθεύδεις; οὐκ ἴσχυσας μίαν ὥραν γρηγορῆσαι;

[30] And Jesus says to him, "Amen! I am saying to you that you yourself today on this night before even the rooster crows twice, three times you will deny me." [31] But he
was speaking excessively, "If it is necessary for me to die with you, I will never ever deny you." Thus, likewise also they all were saying. [32] And they come into an area
where the name is Gethsemane, and he begins saying to his disciples, "Sit here until I pray." [33] And he takes along Peter and James and John with him, he began to be
overwhelmed and to be distressed. [34] And he says to them, "Exceedingly sorrowful is my soul until death; Remain here and keep watchful!" [35] And after going forward a
little, he was falling on the ground, and he was praying in order that, if it were possible, the hour would pass away from him, [36] And he was saying, "Abba, Father, all
things are possible for you; remove this cup from me; but not what I myself want but what you *want*." [37] And he comes and finds them sleeping, and he says to Peter,
"Simon, are you sleeping? Didn't you have strength to keep watch one hour? *Surely, not!*

38 γρηγορεῖτε καὶ προσεύχεσθε, ἵνα μὴ ἔλθητε εἰς πειρασμόν· τὸ μὲν πνεῦμα πρόθυμον ἡ δὲ σὰρξ ἀσθενής.

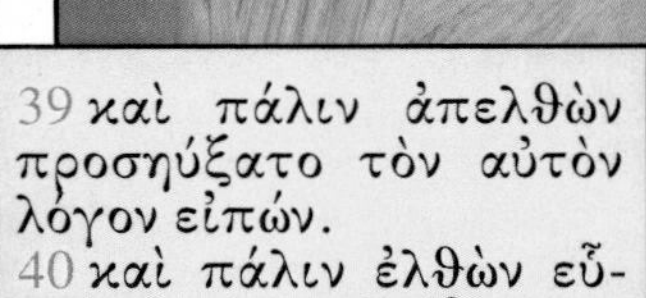
39 καὶ πάλιν ἀπελθὼν προσηύξατο τὸν αὐτὸν λόγον εἰπών.
40 καὶ πάλιν ἐλθὼν εὗρεν αὐτοὺς καθεύδοντας, ἦσαν γὰρ αὐτῶν οἱ ὀφθαλμοὶ καταβαρυνόμενοι, καὶ οὐκ ᾔδεισαν τί ἀποκριθῶσιν αὐτῷ.
41 καὶ ἔρχεται τὸ τρίτον καὶ λέγει αὐτοῖς·

42 Καθεύδετε τὸ λοιπὸν καὶ ἀναπαύεσθε· ἀπέχει· ἦλθεν ἡ ὥρα, ἰδοὺ παραδίδοται ὁ υἱὸς τοῦ ἀνθρώπου εἰς τὰς χεῖρας τῶν ἁμαρτωλῶν.

42 ἐγείρεσθε ἄγωμεν· ἰδοὺ ὁ παραδιδούς με ἤγγικεν.

43 Καὶ εὐθὺς ἔτι αὐτοῦ λαλοῦντος παραγίνεται Ἰούδας εἷς τῶν δώδεκα καὶ μετ᾽ αὐτοῦ ὄχλος μετὰ μαχαιρῶν καὶ ξύλων παρὰ τῶν ἀρχιερέων καὶ τῶν γραμματέων καὶ τῶν πρεσβυτέρων.
44 δεδώκει δὲ ὁ παραδιδοὺς αὐτὸν σύσσημον αὐτοῖς λέγων·
Ὃν ἂν φιλήσω αὐτός ἐστιν· κρατήσατε αὐτὸν καὶ ἀπάγετε ἀσφαλῶς.

45 καὶ ἐλθὼν εὐθὺς προσελθὼν αὐτῷ λέγει·
Ῥαββί.
καὶ κατεφίλησεν αὐτόν.

46 οἱ δὲ ἐπέβαλαν τὰς χεῖρας αὐτῷ καὶ ἐκράτησαν αὐτόν.

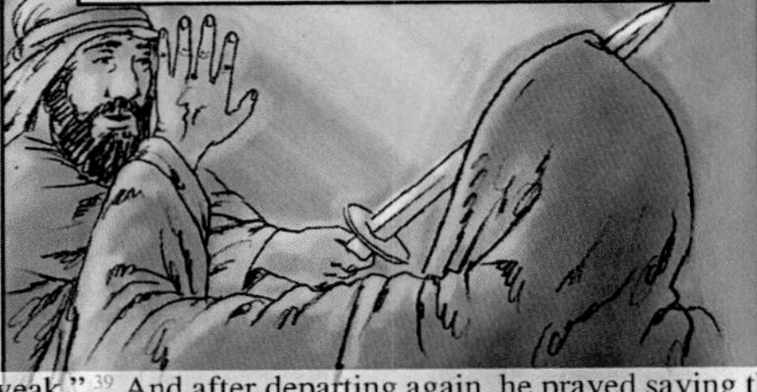
47 εἷς δέ τις τῶν παρεστηκότων σπασάμενος τὴν μάχαιραν ἔπαισεν τὸν δοῦλον τοῦ ἀρχιερέως καὶ ἀφεῖλεν αὐτοῦ τὸ ὠτάριον.

38 You *all* be watchful and be praying, lest you come into temptation; the Spirit indeed is willing but the flesh is weak." 39 And after departing again, he prayed saying the same prayer. 40 And, after coming again, he found them sleeping, for their eyes were weighed down, and they did not know what they should answer back to him. 41 And he comes the third time and says to them, "You are sleeping the remainder *of the night* and resting up; it is enough! The hour came; behold, the Son of Man is being handed over into the hands of sinners! 42 Rise up! Let us go! Behold, the one handing me over has arrived!" 43 And straightaway, while still he was speaking, Judas, one of the twelve, arrives and with him a crowd with swords and clubs from the chief priests and the scribes and the elders. 44 Well, the one handing him over had given them a sign saying, "Whomever I kiss, he is the one. Seize him and be leading him away safely." 45 And, after coming, straightaway approaching him, he says, "Rabbi!" and kissed him. 46 So, they laid hands on him and seized him. 47 But a certain one of the ones standing by, after drawing the sword, struck the servant of the high priest and cut off his ear.

48 καὶ ἀποκριθεὶς ὁ Ἰησοῦς εἶπεν αὐτοῖς·
ς π ηστ ν ἐξήλθατε μετὰ μαχαιρῶν καὶ ξύλων συλλαβεῖν με;
49 καθ᾽ ἡμέραν ἤμην πρὸς ὑμᾶς ἐν τῷ ἱερῷ διδάσκων καὶ οὐκ ἐκρατήσατέ με· ἀλλ᾽ ἵνα πληρωθῶσιν αἱ γραφαί.

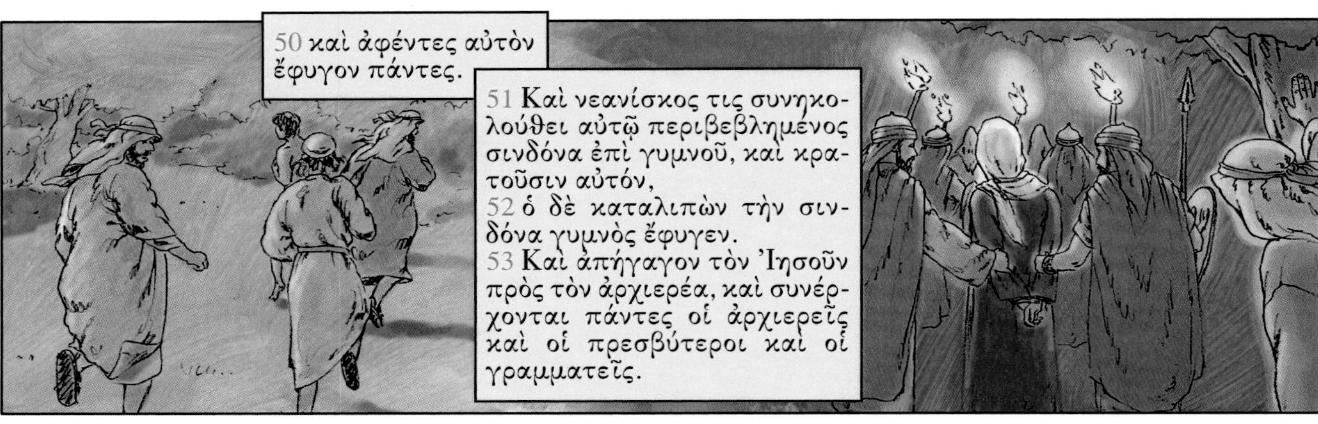
50 καὶ ἀφέντες αὐτὸν ἔφυγον πάντες.
51 Καὶ νεανίσκος τις συνηκολούθει αὐτῷ περιβεβλημένος σινδόνα ἐπὶ γυμνοῦ, καὶ κρατοῦσιν αὐτόν,
52 ὁ δὲ καταλιπὼν τὴν σινδόνα γυμνὸς ἔφυγεν.
53 Καὶ ἀπήγαγον τὸν Ἰησοῦν πρὸς τὸν ἀρχιερέα, καὶ συνέρχονται πάντες οἱ ἀρχιερεῖς καὶ οἱ πρεσβύτεροι καὶ οἱ γραμματεῖς.

54 καὶ ὁ Πέτρος ἀπὸ μακρόθεν ἠκολούθησεν αὐτῷ ἕως ἔσω εἰς τὴν αὐλὴν τοῦ ἀρχιερέως καὶ ἦν συγκαθήμενος μετὰ τῶν ὑπ-ηρετῶν καὶ θερμαινόμενος πρὸς τὸ φῶς.
55 οἱ δὲ ἀρχιερεῖς καὶ ὅλον τὸ συνέδριον ἐζήτουν κατὰ τοῦ Ἰησοῦ μαρτυρίαν εἰς τὸ θανατῶσαι αὐτόν, καὶ οὐχ ηὕ-ρισκον·
56 πολλοὶ γὰρ ἐψευδομαρ-τύρουν κατ᾽ αὐτοῦ, καὶ ἴσαι αἱ μαρτυρίαι οὐκ ἦσαν.
57 καί τινες ἀναστάντες ἐψευδομαρτύρουν κατ᾽ αὐτοῦ λέγοντες
58 ὅτι
Ἡμεῖς ἠκούσαμεν αὐτοῦ λέγοντος ὅτι Ἐγὼ καταλύσω τὸν ναὸν τοῦτον τὸν χειροποίητον καὶ διὰ τριῶν ἡμερῶν ἄλλον ἀχειροποίητον οἰκοδομήσω·
59 καὶ οὐδὲ οὕτως ἴση ἦν ἡ μαρτυρία αὐτῶν.
60 καὶ ἀναστὰς ὁ ἀρχιερεὺς εἰς μέσον ἐπηρώτησεν τὸν Ἰησοῦν λέγων·

[48] And responding back, Jesus said to them, "As if against a bandit you *all* came out with swords and clubs to capture me? [49] Daily I was with you in the temple teaching
and you did not seize me; but *this is being done* in order that that the scriptures would be fulfilled." [50] And leaving him, they all fled. [51] And a certain young man was
following him, having a linen cloth around his naked body, and they grab him; [52] but he, leaving behind the linen cloth, fled naked. [53] And they led Jesus away to the high
priest, and all the chief priests and the elders and the scribes begin gathering together. [54] And Peter followed him from afar, until inside into the courtyard of the high
priest, and he was sitting with the officers and warming himself at the fire. [55] Well, the chief priests and the whole Sanhedrin were seeking a testimony against Jesus in
order to kill him, and they were not finding it. [56] For many were falsely witnessing against him, and the testimonies were not the same. [57] And certain men standing up
were witnessing falsely against him saying [58] this: "We ourselves heard him saying this: 'I myself will destroy this handmade temple and after three days I will build
another not handmade.'" [59] And neither in this way was their testimony the same. [60] And after standing up into the middle, the high priest asked Jesus saying, "Don't you
have some answer back? *Surely, yes!* Why are these men testifying against you?"

Οὐκ ἀποκρίνῃ οὐδέν; τί οὗτοί σου καταμαρτυροῦσιν;
61 ὁ δὲ ἐσιώπα καὶ οὐκ ἀπεκρίνατο οὐδέν. πάλιν ὁ ἀρχιερεὺς ἐπηρώτα αὐτὸν καὶ λέγει αὐτῷ·
Σὺ εἶ ὁ χριστὸς ὁ υἱὸς τοῦ εὐλογητοῦ;

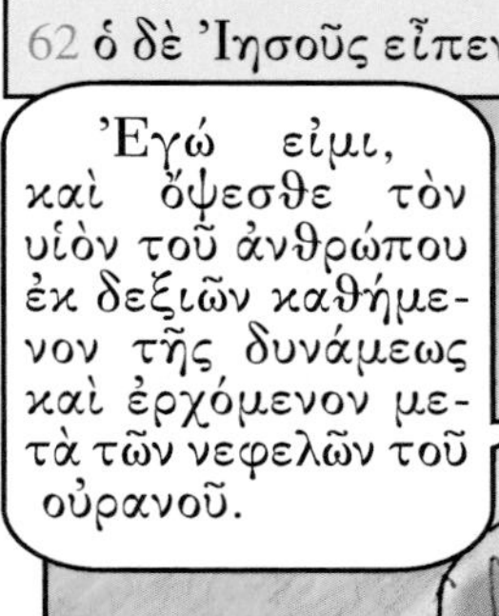
62 ὁ δὲ Ἰησοῦς εἶπεν·
Ἐγώ εἰμι, καὶ ὄψεσθε τὸν υἱὸν τοῦ ἀνθρώπου ἐκ δεξιῶν καθήμενον τῆς δυνάμεως καὶ ἐρχόμενον μετὰ τῶν νεφελῶν τοῦ οὐρανοῦ.

63 ὁ δὲ ἀρχιερεὺς διαρρήξας τοὺς χιτῶνας αὐτοῦ λέγει·
Τί ἔτι χρείαν ἔχομεν μαρτύρων; 64 ἠκούσατε τῆς βλασφημίας· τί ὑμῖν φαίνεται;
οἱ δὲ πάντες κατέκριναν αὐτὸν ἔνοχον εἶναι θανάτου. 65 καὶ ἤρξαντό τινες ἐμπτύειν αὐτῷ

καὶ περικαλύπτειν αὐτοῦ τὸ πρόσωπον καὶ κολαφίζειν αὐτὸν καὶ λέγειν αὐτῷ·
Προφήτευσον.
καὶ οἱ ὑπηρέται ῥαπίσμασιν αὐτὸν ἔλαβον.

66 Καὶ ὄντος τοῦ Πέτρου κάτω ἐν τῇ αὐλῇ ἔρχεται μία τῶν παιδισ-κῶν τοῦ ἀρχιερέως,

67 καὶ ἰδοῦσα τὸν Πέτρον θερμαινόμενον ἐμβλέψασα αὐτῷ λέγει·
Καὶ σὺ μετὰ τοῦ Ναζαρηνοῦ ἦσθα τοῦ Ἰησοῦ·
68 ὁ δὲ ἠρνήσατο λέγων·
Οὔτε οἶδα οὔτε ἐπίσταμαι σὺ τί λέγεις.

καὶ ἐξῆλθεν ἔξω εἰς τὸ προαύλιον καὶ ἀλέκτωρ ἐφώνησεν. 69 καὶ ἡ παιδίσκη ἰδοῦσα αὐτὸν ἤρξατο πάλιν λέγειν τοῖς παρεστῶσιν ὅτι
Οὗτος ἐξ αὐτῶν ἐστιν.

[61] But he was keeping quiet and did not answer back anything. Again the high priest proceeded asking him and says to him, "Are you yourself the Christ, the Son of the Blessed?" [62] So Jesus said, "I myself am *he*, and you will see the Son of Man sitting at the right hand of power and coming with the clouds of heaven." [63] Well, the high priest, after tearing his clothes, says, "What further need do we have for witnesses? [64] You have heard the blasphemy! What is clear to you?" Well, they all condemned him to be worthy of death. [65] And some began to spit on him and to cover his face and to hit him and to say to him, "Prophesy!" and the officers took him with punches. [66] And while Peter was below in the courtyard, one woman of the servants of the high priest comes [67] and, after seeing Peter warming up, staring at him, she says, "You also were with the Nazarene, Jesus." [68] But he denied *it* saying, "Neither do I know nor do I understand what you yourself are saying!" And he departed outside into the porch and a rooster crowed. [69] And the female servant, after seeing him, began again to say to the ones standing by, "This guy is from them!"

70 ὁ δὲ πάλιν ἠρνεῖτο. καὶ μετὰ μικρὸν πάλιν οἱ παρεστῶτες ἔλεγον τῷ Πέτρῳ·
Ἀληθῶς ἐξ αὐτῶν εἶ, καὶ γὰρ Γαλιλαῖος εἶ καὶ ἡ λαλιά σου ὁμοιάζει·
71 ὁ δὲ ἤρξατο ἀναθεματίζειν καὶ ὀμνύναι ὅτι
Οὐκ οἶδα τὸν ἄνθρωπον τοῦτον ὃν λέγετε.
72 καὶ εὐθὺς ἐκ δευτέρου ἀλέκτωρ ἐφώνησεν·

καὶ ἀνεμνήσθη ὁ Πέτρος τὸ ῥῆμα ὡς εἶπεν αὐτῷ ὁ Ἰησοῦς ὅτι
Πρὶν ἀλέκτορα φωνῆσαι δὶς τρίς με ἀπαρνήσῃ.
καὶ ἐπιβαλὼν ἔκλαιεν.

Κεφ.
IF´

1 Καὶ εὐθὺς πρωῒ συμβούλιον ποιήσαντες οἱ ἀρχιερεῖς μετὰ τῶν πρεσβυτέρων καὶ γραμματέων καὶ ὅλον τὸ συνέδριον δήσαντες τὸν Ἰησοῦν ἀπήνεγκαν καὶ παρέδωκαν Πιλάτῳ.
2 καὶ ἐπηρώτησεν αὐτὸν ὁ Πιλᾶτος·
Σὺ εἶ ὁ βασιλεὺς τῶν Ἰουδαίων;
ὁ δὲ ἀποκριθεὶς αὐτῷ λέγει·
Σὺ λέγεις.

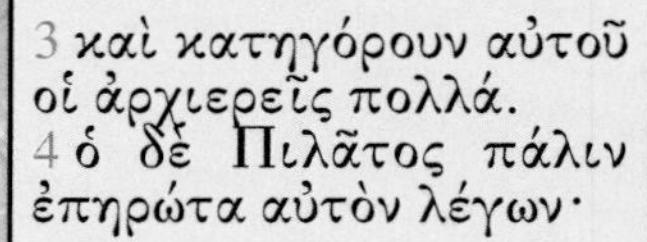
3 καὶ κατηγόρουν αὐτοῦ οἱ ἀρχιερεῖς πολλά.
4 ὁ δὲ Πιλᾶτος πάλιν ἐπηρώτα αὐτὸν λέγων·
Οὐκ ἀποκρίνῃ οὐδέν; ἴδε πόσα σου κατηγοροῦσιν.
5 ὁ δὲ Ἰησοῦς οὐκέτι οὐδὲν ἀπεκρίθη, ὥστε θαυμάζειν τὸν Πιλᾶτον.

6 Κατὰ δὲ ἑορτὴν ἀπέλυεν αὐτοῖς ἕνα δέσμιον ὃν παρῃτοῦντο.
7 ἦν δὲ ὁ λεγόμενος Βαραββᾶς μετὰ τῶν στασιαστῶν δεδεμένος οἵτινες ἐν τῇ στάσει φόνον πεποιήκεισαν.
8 καὶ ἀναβὰς ὁ ὄχλος ἤρξατο αἰτεῖσθαι καθὼς ἐποίει αὐτοῖς.

70 But he again was denying *it*. And after a little while, again the ones standing by were saying to Peter, "Truly you are from them, for you are even a Galilean and your
way of speaking is similar." 71 But he began to curse and to swear this: "I do not know this man about whom you are speaking." 72 And straightaway the second time a
rooster crowed. And Peter remembered the word as Jesus had said to him, "Before the rooster crows twice, three times you will deny me." And breaking down, he was
weeping. 15:1 And straightaway in the morning, the chief priests with the elders and scribes making a council, and the whole Sanhedrin binding Jesus, they carried away
and handed *him* over to Pilate. 2 And Pilate asked him, "Are you yourself the King of the Jews?" So, he, answering back, says to him, "You yourself are saying so." 3 And
the chief priests were accusing him of many things. 4 So, Pilate again kept asking him saying, "You aren't answering back one thing? *Surely, yes!* Look how much they
are accusing you!" 5 Well, Jesus no longer answered back one thing, so that Pilate was marveling. 6 Additionally, at the feast he proceeded releasing to them one prisoner,
whom they were requesting. 7 Moreover, the man was the one called Barabbas, having been bound with the insurrectionists who in the riot had committed murder. 8 And
after going up, the crowd began to ask *for Barabbas*, as he was doing *this release* for them.

9 ιλᾶτος πεκρ η α τοῖς λ

Θέλετε ἀπολύσω ὑμῖν τὸν βασιλέα τῶν Ἰουδαίων;

10 ἐγίνωσκεν γὰρ ὅτι διὰ φθόνον παραδεδώκεισαν αὐτὸν οἱ ἀρχιερεῖς.
11 οἱ δὲ ἀρχιερεῖς ἀνέσεισαν τὸν ὄχλον ἵνα μᾶλλον τὸν Βαραββᾶν ἀπολύσῃ αὐτοῖς.
12 ὁ δὲ Πιλᾶτος πάλιν ἀποκριθεὶς ἔλεγεν αὐτοῖς·

Τί οὖν θέλετε ποιήσω ὃν λέγετε τὸν βασιλέα τῶν Ἰουδαίων;

13 οἱ δὲ πάλιν ἔκραξαν·

Σταύρωσον αὐτόν.

14 ὁ δὲ Πιλᾶτος ἔλεγεν αὐτοῖς·
Τί γὰρ ἐποίησεν κακόν;
οἱ δὲ περισσῶς ἔκραξαν·
Σταύρωσον αὐτόν.
15 ὁ δὲ Πιλᾶτος βουλόμενος τῷ ὄχλῳ τὸ ἱκανὸν ποιῆσαι ἀπέλυσεν αὐτοῖς τὸν Βαραββᾶν, καὶ παρέδωκεν τὸν Ἰησοῦν φραγελλώσας ἵνα σταυρωθῇ.
16 Οἱ δὲ στρατιῶται ἀπήγαγον αὐτὸν ἔσω τῆς αὐλῆς, ὅ ἐστιν πραιτώριον, καὶ συγκαλοῦσιν ὅλην τὴν σπεῖραν.

17 καὶ ἐνδιδύσκουσιν αὐτὸν πορφύραν καὶ περιτιθέασιν αὐτῷ πλέξαντες ἀκάνθινον στέφανον·
18 καὶ ἤρξαντο ἀσπάζεσθαι αὐτόν·

Χαῖρε, βασιλεῦ τῶν Ἰουδαίων·

19 καὶ ἔτυπτον αὐτοῦ τὴν κεφαλὴν καλάμῳ καὶ ἐνέπτυον αὐτῷ, καὶ τιθέντες τὰ γόνατα προσεκύνουν αὐτῷ.

20 καὶ ὅτε ἐνέπαιξαν αὐτῷ, ἐξέδυσαν αὐτὸν τὴν πορφύραν καὶ ἐνέδυσαν αὐτὸν τὰ ἱμάτια τὰ ἴδια. καὶ ἐξάγουσιν αὐτὸν ἵνα σταυρώσωσιν αὐτόν.
21 Καὶ ἀγγαρεύουσιν παράγοντά τινα Σίμωνα Κυρηναῖον ἐρχόμενον ἀπ᾽ ἀγροῦ, τὸν πατέρα Ἀλεξ-άνδρου καὶ Ῥούφου, ἵνα ἄρῃ τὸν σταυρὸν αὐτοῦ.

9 Well, Pilate answered back to them saying, "Do you want that I would release to you the King of the Jews?" 10 For he was realizing that because of envy the chief priests
had handed him over. 11 So, the chief priests stirred up the crowd in order that, instead, he would release Barabbas to them. 12 But, Pilate, again answering back, said to
them, "What, therefore, do you want that I do about him whom you call the King of the Jews?" 13 Well, they again cried out, "Crucify him!" 14 So, Pilate was saying to
them, "What evil did he do?" But they cried out even more, "Crucify him!" 15 Well, Pilate, wishing to do something sufficient for the crowd, released Barabbas to them,
and he handed over Jesus, flogging *him*, in order that he would be crucified. 16 So, the soldiers led him away inside the courtyard, which is the Praetorium, and they begin
calling together the whole cohort. 17 And they begin dressing him with purple and, they put on him, after forming *it*, a thorny crown; 18 and they began to salute him, "Hail,
King of the Jews!" 19 And they were striking his head with a reed and they were spitting on him, and after bowing knees, they were giving homage to him. 20 And when
they had mocked him, they undressed him in the purple and dressed him in his own clothes. And they lead him out in order that they would crucify him. 21 And they force
someone passing by, Simon of Cyrene, coming from the countryside, the father of Alexander and Rufus, in order that he would carry his cross.

22 καὶ φέρουσιν αὐτὸν
ἐπὶ τὸν Γολγοθᾶν τόπον,
ὅ ἐστιν μεθερμηνευόμε-
νον Κρανίου Τόπος.

23 καὶ ἐδίδουν αὐτῷ ἐσμυρνισ-
μένον οἶνον, ὃς δὲ οὐκ ἔλαβεν.
24 καὶ σταυροῦσιν αὐτὸν

22 And they bring him to the place Golgotha, which is translated: 'Place of the Skull.'
23 And they were offering to him myrrh mixed with wine, who, however, did not take
it.
24 And they begin crucifying him and they begin dividing up his clothes, casting lots for them, *to determine* who would take what.

καὶ διαμερίζονται
τὰ ἱμάτια αὐτοῦ,
βάλλοντες κλῆρον
ἐπ' αὐτὰ τίς τί ἄρῃ.

25 Ἦν δὲ ὥρα τρίτη καὶ
ἐσταύρωσαν αὐτόν.
26 καὶ ἦν ἡ ἐπιγραφὴ τῆς
αἰτίας αὐτοῦ ἐπιγεγραμ-
μένη· Ὁ βασιλεὺς τῶν
Ἰουδαίων.

27 καὶ σὺν αὐτῷ σταυροῦσιν
δύο λῃστάς, ἕνα ἐκ δεξιῶν
καὶ ἕνα ἐξ εὐωνύμων αὐτοῦ.
28 [Καὶ ἐπληρώθη ἡ γραφὴ ἡ
λέγουσα, καὶ μετὰ ἀνόμων
ἐλογίσθη.]

25 So, it was the third hour and they crucified him. 26 And the inscription of his charge was written up: THE KING OF THE JEWS. 27 And they kept crucifying with him
two bandits, one on his right and one on his left. 28 *And the scripture was fulfilled that says, "And he was charged with the lawless ones."*

29 Καὶ οἱ παραπορε... ἐβλασφή-
μουν αὐτὸν κινοῦ... κεφαλὰς
αὐτῶν καὶ λέγοντε...
Οὐὰ ὁ καταλύων τὸν ναὸν
καὶ οἰκοδομῶν ἐν τρισὶν ἡμέραις,
30 σῶσον σεαυτὸν καταβὰς ἀπὸ
τοῦ σταυροῦ.
...ἀλλήλους μετὰ τῶν γραμματέων ἔλεγον·
Ἄλλους ἔσωσεν, ἑαυτὸν
οὐ δύναται σῶσαι·
32 ὁ χριστὸς ὁ βασιλεὺς
Ἰσραὴλ καταβάτω νῦν ἀπὸ
τοῦ σταυροῦ, ἵνα ἴδωμεν καὶ
πιστεύσωμεν.
καὶ οἱ συνεσταυρωμένοι
σὺν αὐτῷ ὠνείδιζον αὐτόν.

33 Καὶ γενομένης ὥρας ἕκ-
της σκότος ἐγένετο ἐφ᾽ ὅλην
τὴν γῆν ἕως ὥρας ἐνάτης.
34 καὶ τῇ ἐνάτῃ ὥρᾳ ἐβόησεν
ὁ Ἰησοῦς φωνῇ μεγάλῃ·
Ἐλωῒ ἐλωῒ λεμὰ σαβαχθάνι;
ὅ ἐστιν μεθερμηνευόμενον
Ὁ θεός μου ὁ θεός μου, εἰς τί
ἐγκατέλιπές με;

35 καί τινες τῶν παρεστη-
κότων ἀκούσαντες ἔλεγον·
Ἴδε Ἠλίαν φωνεῖ.

36 δραμὼν δέ τις
καὶ γεμίσας σπόγ-
γον ὄξους περιθεὶς
καλάμῳ ἐπότιζεν
αὐτόν, λέγων·
Ἄφετε
ἴδωμεν εἰ
ἔρχεται Ἠλίας
καθελεῖν αὐτόν.

37 ὁ δὲ Ἰησοῦς ἀφεὶς φωνὴν
μεγάλην ἐξέπνευσεν.

38 καὶ τὸ καταπέτα-
σμα τοῦ ναοῦ ἐσχίσθη
εἰς δύο ἀπ᾽ ἄνωθεν
ἕως κάτω.

39 ἰδὼν δὲ ὁ κεντυρίων ὁ
παρεστηκὼς ἐξ ἐναντίας
αὐτοῦ ὅτι οὕτως ἐξέπνευσεν
εἶπεν·

Ἀληθῶς οὗτος ὁ
ἄνθρωπος υἱὸς θεοῦ ἦν.

40 Ἦσαν δὲ καὶ γυναῖκες
ἀπὸ μακρόθεν θεωροῦσαι,

29 And the ones passing by were insulting him shaking their heads and saying, "Ha! The one destroying the temple and building it in three days, 30 save yourself, *by* coming
down from the cross!" 31 Similarly also, the chief priests, while mocking among themselves with the scribes, were saying, "Others he saved; himself he is not able to save!
32 Let the Christ, the King of Israel, come down now from the cross, in order that we would see and believe." And the ones being crucified with him were insulting him.
33 And after the sixth hour came, a darkness occurred upon the whole land until the ninth hour. 34 And at the ninth hour Jesus cried with a loud voice, "Eloi, Eloi, lema
savakhthani," which is translated: 'My God, my God, why did you abandon me?'" 35 And some of the ones standing nearby, after hearing, were saying, "Behold, he is
calling Elijah!" 36 So, someone running and filling a sponge full of vinegar, putting *it* on a stick, was giving him it to drink saying, "You *all* move away! Let us see if Elijah
comes to take him down!" 37 Well, Jesus, after releasing a great sound, expired. 38 And the veil of the temple was torn into two from up top to bottom. 39 Well, after the
centurion standing by across from him saw that he had expired in this way, he said, "Truly this very person was the Son of God!" 40 Now, there were also women watching
from a distance, among whom were Mary Magdalene and Mary the *mother* of James the younger and of Joses, and Salome,

ἐν αἷς καὶ Μαρία ἡ
Μαγδαληνὴ καὶ Μαρία
ἡ Ἰακώβου τοῦ μικροῦ
καὶ Ἰωσῆτος μήτηρ καὶ
Σαλώμη,
41 αἳ ὅτε ἦν ἐν τῇ Γα-
λιλαίᾳ ἠκολούθουν αὐ-
τῷ καὶ διηκόνουν αὐτῷ,
καὶ ἄλλαι πολλαὶ αἱ
συναναβᾶσαι αὐτῷ εἰς
Ἱεροσόλυμα.

42 Καὶ ἤδη ὀψίας γενομένης, ἐπεὶ
ἦν παρασκευή, ὅ ἐστιν προσάββα-
τον,
43 ἐλθὼν Ἰωσὴφ ὁ ἀπὸ Ἁριμα-
θαίας εὐσχήμων βουλευτής, ὃς καὶ
αὐτὸς ἦν προσδεχόμενος τὴν βασιλείαν τοῦ θεοῦ, τολμήσας
εἰσῆλθεν πρὸς τὸν Πιλᾶτον καὶ
ᾐτήσατο τὸ σῶμα τοῦ Ἰησοῦ.

44 ὁ δὲ Πιλᾶτος ἐθαύμασεν
εἰ ἤδη τέθνηκεν, καὶ προ-
σκαλεσάμενος τὸν κεντυ-
ρίωνα ἐπηρώτησεν αὐτὸν εἰ
πάλαι ἀπέθανεν·
45 καὶ γνοὺς ἀπὸ τοῦ κεντυ-
ρίωνος ἐδωρήσατο τὸ πτῶμα
τῷ Ἰωσήφ.
46 καὶ ἀγοράσας σινδόνα
καθελὼν αὐτὸν ἐνείλησεν τῇ
σινδόνι καὶ ἔθηκεν αὐτὸν ἐν
μνημείῳ ὃ ἦν λελατομημέ-
νον ἐκ πέτρας,

καὶ προσεκύλισεν λί-θον ἐπὶ τὴν θύραν τοῦ μνημείου.
47 ἡ δὲ Μαρία ἡ Μαγδαληνὴ καὶ Μαρία ἡ Ἰωσῆτος ἐθεώρουν
ποῦ τέθειται.

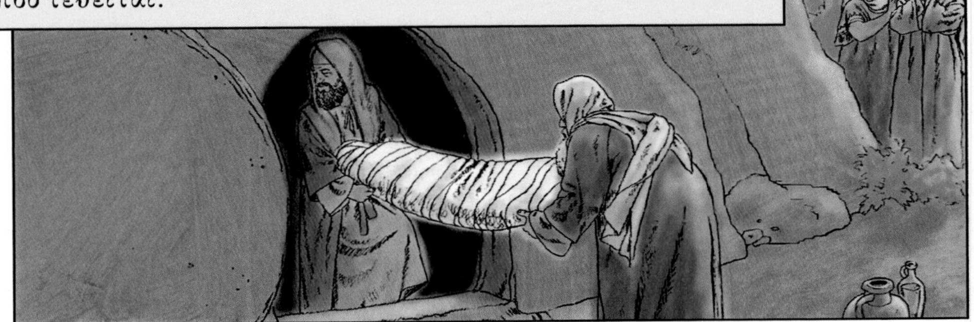

Κεφ.
ΙΖ´

1 Καὶ διαγενομένου τοῦ σαββάτου Μαρία ἡ Μαγδαληνὴ καὶ
Μαρία ἡ τοῦ Ἰακώβου καὶ Σαλώμη ἠγόρασαν ἀρώματα ἵνα
ἐλθοῦσαι ἀλείψωσιν αὐτόν.
2 καὶ λίαν πρωῒ τῇ μιᾷ τῶν σαβ-
βάτων ἔρχονται ἐπὶ τὸ μνημεῖον
ἀνατείλαντος τοῦ ἡλίου.
3 καὶ ἔλεγον πρὸς ἑαυτάς·

Τίς ἀποκυλίσει ἡμῖν
τὸν λίθον ἐκ τῆς θύρας
τοῦ μνημείου;

4 καὶ ἀναβλέψασαι θεωροῦσιν ὅτι
ἀποκεκύλισται ὁ λίθος, ἦν γὰρ
μέγας σφόδρα.

41 who, when he was in Galilee, were following him and were ministering to him, and *there were* many other women coming up with him into Jerusalem. 42 And after
evening had come, since it was the Preparation Day, that is, the day before the Sabbath, 43 after coming, Joseph of Arimathaea, a prominent member of the council, who
also himself was awaiting the Kingdom of God, dared enter to Pilate and he asked for the body of Jesus. 44 Well, Pilate wondered if he had already died, and after calling
to the centurion, he asked him if he had died just then. 45 And, after learning from the centurion, he granted the corpse to Joseph. 46 And after buying a linen cloth, taking
him down, he wrapped *him* in the linen cloth and laid him in a tomb, which had been cut out of a rock, and he rolled a stone against the door of the tomb. 47 Moreover,
Mary Magdalene and Mary, the *mother* of Joses, were watching where he had been laid. 16:1 And after the Sabbath passed, Mary Magdalene and Mary, the *mother* of
James, and Salome, bought spices in order that, after coming, they would anoint him. 2 And very early on the first day of the week, they begin going to the tomb, after the
sun arose. 3 And they were saying among themselves, "Who will roll away for us the stone from the door of the tomb? 4 And after looking up, they see that the stone had
been rolled away, for it was very large.

5 καὶ εἰσελθοῦσαι εἰς τὸ μνημεῖον εἶδον νεανίσκον καθήμενον ἐν τοῖς δεξιοῖς περιβεβλημένον στολὴν λευκήν, καὶ ἐξεθαμβήθησαν.
6 ὁ δὲ λέγει αὐταῖς·

Μὴ ἐκθαμβεῖσθε· Ἰησοῦν ζητεῖτε τὸν Ναζαρηνὸν τὸν ἐσταυρωμένον· ἠγέρθη, οὐκ ἔστιν ὧδε· ἴδε, ὁ τόπος ὅπου ἔθηκαν αὐτόν·
7 ἀλλὰ ὑπάγετε εἴπατε τοῖς μαθηταῖς αὐτοῦ καὶ τῷ Πέτρῳ ὅτι Προάγει ὑμᾶς εἰς τὴν Γαλιλαίαν· ἐκεῖ αὐτὸν ὄψεσθε, καθὼς εἶπεν ὑμῖν.

8 καὶ ἐξελθοῦσαι ἔφυγον ἀπὸ τοῦ μνημείου, εἶχεν γὰρ αὐτὰς τρόμος καὶ ἔκστασις· καὶ οὐδενὶ οὐδὲν εἶπαν, ἐφοβοῦντο γάρ. [[Πάντα δὲ τὰ παρηγγελμένα τοῖς περὶ τὸν Πέτρον συντόμως ἐξήγγειλαν. μετὰ δὲ ταῦτα καὶ αὐτὸς ὁ Ἰησοῦς ἀπὸ ἀνατολῆς καὶ ἄχρι δύσεως ἐξαπέστειλεν δι᾽ αὐτῶν τὸ ἱερὸν καὶ ἄφθαρτον κήρυγμα τῆς αἰωνίου σωτηρίας. ἀμήν.]

9 Ἀναστὰς δὲ πρωῒ πρώτῃ σαββάτου ἐφάνη πρῶτον Μαρίᾳ τῇ Μαγδαληνῇ, παρ᾽ ἧς ἐκβεβλήκει ἑπτὰ δαιμόνια.

10 ἐκείνη πορευθεῖσα ἀπήγγειλεν τοῖς μετ᾽ αὐτοῦ γενομένοις πενθοῦσι καὶ κλαίουσιν·
11 κἀκεῖνοι ἀκούσαντες ὅτι ζῇ καὶ ἐθεάθη ὑπ᾽ αὐτῆς ἠπίστησαν.

12 Μετὰ δὲ ταῦτα δυσὶν ἐξ αὐτῶν περιπατοῦσιν ἐφανερώθη ἐν ἑτέρᾳ μορφῇ πορευομένοις εἰς ἀγρόν·

13 κἀκεῖνοι ἀπελθόντες ἀπήγγειλαν τοῖς λοιποῖς· οὐδὲ ἐκείνοις ἐπίστευσαν.

5 And after entering into the tomb, they saw a young man sitting on the right side wrapped around in a white robe, and they were alarmed. 6 Well, he says to them, “Do
not be alarmed! You are seeking for Jesus, the Nazarene, who has been crucified. He was raised up; he is not here! Look, the place where they laid him! 7 But go, speak
to his disciples and to Peter this: ‘He is going ahead of you *all* into Galilee; there you will see him, just as he said to you.’” 8 And after going out, they fled from the tomb,
for shaking and bewilderment was holding them; and to no one did they speak anything, for they were being afraid. Well, all that had been commanded they reported concisely to the ones around Peter. Moreover, after these things, even Jesus himself sent out through them from east and as far as the west the sacred and undying message of
everlasting salvation. Amen! 9 So, after arising early on the first day of the week, he appeared first to Mary Magdalene, from whom he had cast out seven demons. 10 That
one, after going, reported to the ones being with him, while they were mourning and weeping. 11 And these ones, after hearing that he was alive and he had been seen by
her, did not believe. 12 Then, after these events, to two of them while they were walking he appeared in another form in a field; 13 And these ones, after departing, reported
to the rest; but neither did they believe those ones.

14 Ὕστερον δὲ ἀνακειμένοις αὐτοῖς τοῖς ἕνδεκα ἐφανερώθη, καὶ ὠνείδισεν τὴν ἀπιστίαν αὐτῶν καὶ σκληροκαρδίαν ὅτι τοῖς θεασαμένοις αὐτὸν ἐγηγερμένον οὐκ ἐπίστευσαν.

15 καὶ εἶπεν αὐτοῖς·

Πορευθέντες εἰς τὸν κόσμον ἅπαντα κηρύξατε τὸ εὐαγγέλιον πάσῃ τῇ κτίσει.
16 ὁ πιστεύσας καὶ βαπτισθεὶς σωθήσεται, ὁ δὲ ἀπιστήσας κατακριθήσεται.

17 σημεῖα δὲ τοῖς πιστεύσασιν ταῦτα παρακολουθήσει, ἐν τῷ ὀνόματί μου δαιμόνια ἐκβαλοῦσιν, γλώσσαις λαλήσουσιν καιναῖς,

18 ὄφεις ἀροῦσιν κἂν θανάσιμόν τι πίωσιν οὐ μὴ αὐτοὺς βλάψῃ, ἐπὶ ἀρρώστους χεῖρας ἐπιθήσουσιν καὶ καλῶς ἕξουσιν.

19 Ὁ μὲν οὖν κύριος Ἰησοῦς μετὰ τὸ λαλῆσαι αὐτοῖς ἀνελήμφθη εἰς τὸν οὐρανὸν καὶ ἐκάθισεν ἐκ δεξιῶν τοῦ θεοῦ.
20 ἐκεῖνοι δὲ ἐξελθόντες ἐκήρυξαν πανταχοῦ, τοῦ κυρίου συνεργοῦντος καὶ τὸν λόγον βεβαιοῦντος διὰ τῶν ἐπακολουθούντων σημείων.]

[14] Well afterward, to the eleven, while they themselves were reclining, he reproached their unbelief and hardheartedness, because they did not believe the ones seeing him
after having been raised. [15] And he said to them, "Going into the entire world, preach the gospel to all the creation! [16] The one believing and being baptized will be saved,
but the one disbelieving will be condemned. [17] Moreover, these signs will accompany the ones believing: in my name demons they will cast out, with new tongues they
will speak, [18] serpents they will pick up, and, if something deadly they drink, it will never ever hurt them; upon the sick they will lay hands and they will be well."
[19] Therefore, on the one hand, the Lord Jesus, after he spoke to them, was taken up into heaven and sat down at the right hand of God. [20] But, on the other hand, those ones,
after going out, preached everywhere, while the Lord works with *them* and confirms the word through the accompanying signs.

18006443R00053

Made in the USA
San Bernardino, CA
23 December 2014